T0330379

The Economics of Primary Commodities

The Economics of Primary Commodities

Models, Analysis and Policy

Edited by
David Sapsford and Wyn Morgan

Edward Elgar

Published by
Edward Elgar Publishing Limited
Gower House
Croft Road
Aldershot
Hants GU11 3HR
England

Edward Elgar Publishing Company
Old Post Road
Brookfield
Vermont 05036
USA

British Library Cataloguing in Publication Data
Economics of Primary Commodities: Models, Analysis and Policy
  I. Sapsford, David   II. Morgan, Wyn
  382.4

Library of Congress Cataloguing in Publication Data

The Economics of primary commodities: models, analysis and policy/
  edited by David Sapsford and Wyn Morgan.
     p. cm.
  Proceedings of a conference held at Lancaster University's Lakeland campus at Ambleside, May 24–26, 1993.
    1. Primary commodities—Prices—Congresses. 2. Primary commodities—Prices—Econometric models—Congresses.
  I. Sapsford, David. II. Morgan, Wyn.
  HF1040.7.E28 1995
  332.63'28—dc20

                              94–12018
                                 CIP

ISBN 1 85898 029 1

Printed in Great Britain at the University Press, Cambridge

Contents

Contributors

John-ren Chen, Professor of Economics, University of Innsbruck, Austria.

C.T. Ennew, Reader in the School of Management and Finance, University of Nottingham, UK.

A.J. Hughes Hallett, Professor of Economics, University of Strathclyde, UK and Visiting Professor of Economics, Princeton University, US.

S.J. Leybourne, Lecturer in Econometrics, University of Nottingham, UK.

T.A. Lloyd, Lecturer in Economics, University of Nottingham, UK.

Matthias Lutz, Fellow, Institute of Development Studies, University of Sussex, UK.

Alfred Maizels, Senior Fellow, Queen Elizabeth House, Oxford University, UK.

Wyn Morgan, Lecturer in Economics, University of Nottingham, UK.

A.J. Rayner, Professor of Agricultural Economics, University of Nottingham, UK.

G.V. Reed, Senior Lecturer in Economics, University of Nottingham, UK.

David Sapsford, Professor of Economics, Lancaster University, UK.

Prabirjit Sarkar, Professor of Economics, Centre for Studies in Social Science, Calcutta, India.

Sir Hans Singer, Professorial Fellow, Institute of Development Studies, University of Sussex, UK.

Acknowledgements

We would like to express our gratitude to the Potato Marketing Board for its financial support. In addition we would like to express our thanks to our respective secretaries: Anne Stubbins, Penny Sallis and Sue Berry, without whose efforts and cheerfulness the conference and these proceedings would never have materialized. Thanks are also due to Jo Morgan for her enthusiastic help in proof reading and indexing the book.

Preface

The essays in this volume form the proceedings of a conference that was organized jointly by the Economics Department at the University of Lancaster and the University of Nottingham's Centre for Research in Economic Development and International Trade. This conference was held at Lancaster University's Lakeland campus at Ambleside between 24–26 May 1993. The economics of primary commodity markets is a topic of wide appeal and analytical diversity and in putting together the conference programme we were particularly concerned to invite a range of contributions that fully reflects this richness and diversity. As convenors of the conference, we would like to express our gratitude to the contributors to the conference – both the authors of the papers and the conference participants – for responding so effectively and enthusiastically to our invitation to meet this challenge.

The economics of primary commodities is a rapidly developing field of enquiry. We hope that the essays contained in this volume will not only provide readers with an overview of the current 'state of the art' but also with a useful platform from which future research might be launched.

David Sapsford and Wyn Morgan
Lancaster and Nottingham

1. Introduction

David Sapsford and Wyn Morgan

A commodity is something that hurts when you drop it on your big toe, or smells bad if you leave it out in the sun too long.
(*Barron's* 27 June 1983; cited by Maddala, 1990, p. 21)

1.1 BACKGROUND

Although unconventional, the preceding definition of a commodity is useful. Primary commodities – more conventionally defined as food, raw materials, fuels and base metals – have in the past, and indeed still continue to account for a high proportion of the exports of many developing countries. Primary commodities account for over 40 per cent of world trade and World Bank data reveal that of the 42 countries with a per capita GNP of less than (US) $1,600 in 1986, 20 were more than 70 per cent dependent on just two primary commodities for their export earnings. Accordingly, fluctuations in primary commodity export earnings have the potential to disrupt, perhaps severely, the economic stability of less developed countries, their domestic macroeconomic policies and to interrupt the flow of finance for development.

It is important, however, to recognize that primary products are also a major source of export earnings for developed countries. This is illustrated by International Monetary Fund data (IMF 1981, 1984) which indicates that in 1981, 70 per cent of the world's 125 largest economies depended on primary commodities for in excess of 50 per cent of their export earnings, while 43 per cent relied on primaries for more than 75 per cent of their export earnings. Primary commodities, as raw material inputs into the manufacturing sector of the world economy, also play a major role in the behaviour of inflation in the industrialized economies of the world (Bloch and Sapsford, 1992).

The economic analysis of the workings of primary commodity markets is an area of considerable interest from the viewpoints of academic researchers, policy-makers and market participants alike. There are several reasons for this, two of which are as follows. First, as already noted, primary products are extremely important in the context of world trade in general, and in the trading activities of developing countries in particular. Second, there is the fact that for various well-known reasons (see, for example, Singer, 1986) the quantities traded of most primary commodities tend to grow less rapidly than those of other goods (with the consequence that the value of primary trade is more heavily influenced by price movements than is the value of trade in other goods). Accordingly, the determinants of primary commodity prices, and of the terms on which primaries (including those exported by less developed countries) are traded for manufactured goods, are topics of some considerable importance. It is these and related issues which form the subject matter of this book.

1.2   A CRISIS?

The 1980s was a difficult decade for primary commodity producers. Deflating nominal commodity prices by the price of manufactured goods to obtain the commodity terms of trade (as a measure of the real price of primary commodities) we see that (non-oil) commodity price movements during the decade of the 1980s differed markedly from those evident during the earlier post-war decades. In Chapter 2 Alfred Maizels shows that there was a dramatic deterioration during the 1980s in the trend path followed by real commodity prices, a deterioration which appears to have continued into the early 1990s. According to Maizel's calculations, the real price of primary commodities fell at a trend rate of 4.5 per cent per annum during the period 1980 to 1991, a figure which compares with an upward trend of about 1 per cent per year over the period 1962 to 1980. These figures refer to a composite price index covering a wide range of primary commodities and if we unscramble this into broad commodity groups we see more dramatically the nature of real price movements experienced by

particular primary commodity producers and commodity exporting nations during the 1980s. For example, the corresponding trend
rates of decline were 8.9 and 7.4 per cent per annum for *tropical
beverages* and *vegetable oilseeds and oils* respectively. Maizels
points out that by 1990 real commodity prices had fallen to 45 per
cent below their 1980 value and, looking further back in time, he
also notes that in 1990 real prices stood more than 10 per cent
below their 1932 level! Accordingly Maizels, and others, see
commodity markets as being in a state of acute crisis, a crisis which
Maizels argues in Chapter 2 is likely to persist as we move into the
new century unless current national *and* international policies are
reformed. The implications of the 'crisis hypothesis' are explored in
depth by Maizels who points out that the deteriorating trend in
real commodity prices exerts significant adverse effects not only
upon the developing countries but also upon the developed ones.

1.3 CO-MOVEMENT AND STABILIZATION

While Maizels's paper highlights the problems caused, and the
policy challenges raised, by the persistent downward trend in real
commodity prices it should not be forgotten that there exists a large
body of literature that suggests the fluctuations in primary prices
(especially as these feed into fluctuations in export earnings) have
the potential to exert a marked influence upon the economic performance of developing countries (e.g. MacBean and Nguyen, 1988;
Greenway and Sapsford, 1994). One important aspect of this
literature, the so called *excess co-movement hypothesis*, is explored in
Chapter 3 by Steve Leybourne, Tim Lloyd and Geoff Reed. The
basic notion here is quite simply that the prices of different primary
commodities appear in practice to move more closely in unison with
one another than would be expected on the basis of influences that
are common to all commodities. Stated differently, why is it that
primary commodity prices remain correlated with one another even
after accounting for price movements that are attributable to
common macroeconomic factors? In their chapter Leybourne,
Lloyd and Reed critically appraise the existing empirical evidence
relating to the excess co-movement hypothesis and review the expla-
nations previously put forward to account for this phenomenon:
principally the presence of herd (or sympathetic speculative buying)

behaviour, compounded by liquidity effects of various sorts. This re-appraisal of the existing literature reveals some potentially serious shortcomings in the previous approaches used to test the hypothesis. The authors develop a formalized framework to test the co-movement hypothesis in an attempt to explore methodological rather than empirical matters. The provision of specific definitions of co-movement and excess movement provides a logical division between short- and long-run behaviour, an essential aspect for studying price movement as it reduces the cases of spurious co-movement. The authors do, however, recognize the fact that their views have yet to be tested empirically and acknowledge that more research needs to be undertaken in order to establish the validity, or otherwise, of the excess co-movement hypothesis.

Central in the primary commodity economics literature is the question of how policies designed to stabilize the earnings of primary commodity producers in the face of volatile commodity prices might best be constructed and implemented. This theme, introduced in Chapter 2, is explored in detail by Andrew Hughes Hallett in Chapter 4. Hughes Hallett develops an elegant model of the distribution of earnings in a commodity market in which both production and prices are subject to uncertainty. Taking as its starting point the Deaton and Laroque (1992) model, which places emphasis upon the importance of asymmetries in the levels of stocks held in explaining asymmetries in the distribution of commodity prices, Hughes Hallett's paper uses a flexible distributional form in order to derive the associated revenue functions. Using this framework, Hughes Hallett compares the performance of two standard intervention approaches; price stabilization schemes and controls on production, and provides empirical evidence relating to the markets for copper, coffee and rubber. The analysis of this chapter demonstrates that both schemes involve a trade-off, under which improved earnings stability is achieved at the cost of lower expected earnings. However, Hughes Hallett's model suggests that the terms of this trade-off are more favourable under price stabilization in two senses; first, that such schemes typically require smaller interventions in order to achieve a given level of stability and second, that under such schemes the probability that producers will face either low earnings or larger disturbances to earnings is reduced. This is an important result from the policy perspective.

1.4 COMMODITY TERMS OF TRADE

As already noted, the ratio of the price of primary commodities to the price of manufactured goods may be seen as either the commodity terms of trade (or more formally, as the net barter terms of trade between primary commodities and manufacturers) or as a measure of the real price of primary commodities. An important hypothesis in the primary commodities literature was put forward by both Prebisch (1950) and Singer (1950). According to this hypothesis, the net barter terms of trade between primary commodities and manufactured goods had been, and could be expected to continue to be, subject to a declining long-run trend. Although more than 40 years have elapsed since this hypothesis was first put forward the direction and magnitude of the long-run trend in the terms of trade between primary products and manufactured goods is a topic that continues to attract considerable research attention (e.g. Grilli and Yang, 1988; Cuddington and Urzua, 1989, Sapsford *et al.*, 1992). In Chapter 5, Prabirjit Sarkar develops a North–South model that is in the spirit of Kaldor (1976) and uses this framework to explore the various hypotheses put forward by Prebisch, Singer and others to explain the presence of a deteriorating long-run trend in the price of primary commodities relative to manufactured goods. Much of the recent literature relating to the declining long-run trend in the commodity terms of trade has been almost exclusively statistical in character, focusing on the sensitivity of the empirical support for the hypothesis to alternative data sets, alternative estimation techniques, the presence (or otherwise) of unit roots and to the precise path followed by real commodity prices during the early 1920s. Accordingly, Sarkar's theoretical contribution to the literature is to be especially welcomed. Essentially, Sarkar demonstrates how long-run decline in the terms of trade between the (commodity producing) South and the (manufacturing countries of the) North can arise, in a dynamic world where technical progress occurs in both sectors, from shifts in Northern market structure away from competition towards monopoly. While the trend rate of decline may be strengthened by the existence of rising monopoly power and/or rising mark-ups in the North, Sarkar's model suggests that neither factor is a necessary ingredient when explaining the existence of a declining trend.

Hans Singer's joint paper with Matthias Lutz (Chapter 6) deals with a previously neglected topic in the commodity and terms of trade literatures; namely, the consequences of terms of trade volatility, as distinct from those of their trend effect. This chapter directs its attention to the influence that volatile terms of trade might exert upon output growth. Singer and Lutz discuss several channels through which terms of trade volatility might affect growth performance and present a cross-section econometric analysis that employs the conventional production function methodology. The results of this empirical analysis offer some support for the hypothesis that volatile terms of trade exert a downward influence upon output growth. Interestingly, it appears to be the case that the higher-income countries in the sample are the ones that are most adversely affected by terms of trade volatility.

1.5   SPECIFIC COMMODITIES

Much can be learned from the study of particular primary commodity markets as is illustrated by both John-ren Chen's study of the Taiwanese rice market and the study of the British potato market by Wyn Morgan, Tony Rayner and Christine Ennew. In Chapter 7, Chen specifies and estimates a model that is designed to encompass the range of different policies implemented by the Taiwanese authorities over various sub-periods since the 1950's with the objective of influencing price and production behaviour. One notable feature of the Taiwanese rice market is the fact that it is closed, in the sense that private foreign trade in rice is not permitted. Although this characteristic inevitably restricts the extent to which Chen's findings might be generalized to other commodity markets, the closed nature of this particular market enables Chen to clearly identify a series of important domestic, including policy, determinants of rice prices. In Chapter 8, Morgan, Rayner and Ennew analyse the volatility of price in the British potato market between 1969 and 1991. This period encompasses two major changes that may have exerted a direct impact on price volatility in a market characterized by inelastic demand and variable supply. First, free trade was introduced in 1979 after almost 40 years of autarchic supply control by the Potato Marketing Board. Second, in 1980 the London Potato Futures Market (LPFM) was established, with the aim of providing a non-interventionist means of reducing risk and uncertainty faced by individual growers and traders. In Chapter 8 the authors show that, subject to some caveats, the LPFM achieved a degree of success in reducing risk and price uncertainty and argue that in general, futures markets may provide an attractive non-interventionist option for policy makers in the context of other soft-commodity markets.

The economic analysis of primary commodity markets and policies is an important area from both the analytical and policy perspectives. It is hoped that the selection of papers presented in this book will prove useful to both academic researchers and practitioners alike, and that they will serve to stimulate further research in this field.

REFERENCES

Bloch, H. and D. Sapsford (1992): 'Postwar movements in prices of primary products and manufactured goods', *Journal of Post Keynesian Economics*, **14** (2), 249–66.

Cuddington, J. and C. Urzua (1989): 'Trends and cycles in the net barter terms of trade: a new approach', *Economic Journal*, **99** (396), 426–42.

Deaton, A. and G. Laroque (1992): 'On the behaviour of commodity prices', *Review of Economic Studies*, **59** (1), 1–24.

Greenaway, D. and D. Sapsford (1994): 'Exports, growth and liberalisation: an evaluation', *Journal of Policy Modeling*, **16** (2), 165–86.

Grilli, E. and M. Yang (1988): 'Primary commodity prices, manufactured goods prices and the terms of trade of developing countries: what the long run shows', *World Bank Economic Review*, **2** (1), 1–47.

International Monetary Fund (1981): *International Financial Statistics, Annual Supplement*, no. 4 (Washington DC: IMF).

International Monetary Fund (1984), *International Financial Statistics*, Dec. (Washington DC: IMF).

Kaldor, N. (1976): 'Inflation and recession in the world economy', *Economic Journal*, **86** (344), 703–14.

MacBean, A. and D.T. Nguyen (1988): 'Export instability and growth performance', in D. Greenaway (ed.), *Economic Development and International Trade* (London: Macmillan), 95–116.

Maddala, G. (1990): 'Estimation of dynamic disequilibrium models with rational expectations: the case of commodity markets', in L.A. Winters and D. Sapsford (eds), *Primary Commodity Prices: Economic Models and Policy* (Cambridge University Press), 21–37.

Prebisch, R. (1950): 'The economic development of Latin America and its principal problems' (New York: United Nations ECLA); also published in *Economic Bulletin for Latin America* (1962), **7** (1), 1–22.

Sapsford, D., P. Sarkar and H. Singer (1992): 'The Prebisch–Singer terms of trade controversy revisited', *Journal of International Development*, **4**

(3), 315–32.

Singer, H. (1950): 'The distribution of gains between investing and borrowing countries', *American Economic Review (Papers and Proceedings)*, **40**, 473–85.

—— (1986): 'Terms of trade and economic development', in J. Eatwell, M. Milgate and P. Newman (eds), *The New Palgrave: A Dictionary of Economics* (London: Macmillan), 626–8

2. Commodities in Crisis

Alfred Maizels

2.1 BACKGROUND

Over the entire postwar academic discussion of the 'commodity problem',[1] the focus of attention has predominantly been on short-term instability in commodity prices, and commodity export earnings of developing countries, and on the effects of such instability on these countries' economic growth. An associated area of concern has been whether or not there has been a significant downward trend over the long term in the 'real' prices of primary commodities, or in the terms of trade of developing countries in their exchanges with developed countries.

The predominance of the instability issue over that of the long-term trend was, perhaps, due largely to the academic criticisms of the statistical basis of the terms of trade deterioration thesis advanced by Prebisch (1950) and Singer (1950), though more recent analyses have generally supported the deterioration thesis.[2] Intergovernmental consideration of commodity problems has also focused predominantly, though not exclusively, on short-term instability and on measures to reduce instability or to offset its effects on the economies of developing countries. Up to fairly recent years, the negotiation of international commodity agreements – such as those for cocoa, coffee, rubber, sugar and tin – was a recognition of the need to reduce excessive short-term commodity price instability in the interests of the producing countries. The need to offset the adverse effects of commodity export instability was also recognized in the Compensatory Finance Facility of the IMF and in the STABEX scheme of the European Community.

One of the arguments advanced in the present paper is that the balance between the instability problem and the trend problem has

9

changed since the early 1980s, and that consequently the focus of analysis, and of international policy relating to commodities, needs to be shifted accordingly.

A second issue discussed in this paper relates to the perceived wisdom of assuming that short-term commodity market instability, and/or a deterioration in the trend of real commodity prices, are problems only for commodity-dependent developing countries. The argument advanced here is that commodity instability and a deteriorating trend in real commodity prices have significant adverse effects for the developed countries also. Section 2 considers the shift in the 'balance' between short-term and long-term problems and the implications for policy, while Section 3 discusses the impact of instability on the economies of developed countries. Some concluding remarks are provided in Section 4.

2.2 SHORT TERM INSTABILITY AND LONG-TERM TRENDS

The statistical evidence indicates that whereas the degree of short-term instability in prices of primary commodities was somewhat lower in the 1980s than in earlier postwar decades, there was a dramatic deterioration, over the 1980s, in the trend of real commodity prices, a deterioration which appears to have continued into the early 1990s (Table 2.1).

Though overall price instability appears to have declined somewhat since the price 'shocks' of the 1970s, there are none the less a number of commodities of great importance to developing countries' export earnings, for which price instability has remained extremely high. For example, sugar, several vegetable oils and a number of non-ferrous metals had instability indices in the 1980–91 period of more than double the average index for all commodities. The instability problem thus remains a real and important one.

However, the decline in real commodity prices since the early 1980s has been so sharp as to constitute a phenomenon not seen since the Great Depression of the 1930s. According to Grilli-Yang (1988) their commodity price index, which goes up to 1986, that year was the first postwar year in which real commodity prices breached the 1930s nadir (which was reached in 1932). Real commodity prices fell further in 1987, staged a modest recovery in 1988 and 1989,

Table 2.1 *Instability and trends in prices of non-oil commodities exported by developing countries: 1962–91*

	Weight	Instability index[a] 1962–80	Instability index[a] 1980–91	Real price trend (% pa)[b] 1962–80	Real price trend (% pa)[b] 1980–91
Food	42.7	24.8	20.9	1.1	−5.4
Tropical beverages	17.4	25.5	14.0	2.9	−8.9
Vegetable oilseeds and oils	7.0	22.2	16.4	0.2	−7.4
Agricultural raw materials	13.3	16.6	9.0	0.5	−2.3
Minerals, ores and metals	19.7	12.3	15.3	−0.5	−1.3
Total	100.0	15.2	13.0	1.1	−4.5

Sources: UNCTAD *Commodity Yearbook*, 1989 and 1992 (New York: UN).

(a)   Mean percentage deviation from exponential trend.
(b)   Prices in current US dollars deflated by the UN index of export unit value of manufactured goods exported by developed market-economy countries. Trend percentages derived from semi-log regressions of price indices on time.

before falling again in 1990 to 45 per cent below the 1980 level (and over 10 per cent below that for 1932). The outlook for commodity prices over the rest of the 1990s and into the first decade of the next century remains gloomy, at least on the assumption that present national and international policies continue unchanged.[3]

The sharp deterioration in the commodity terms of trade in the 1980s has involved a massive loss in export earnings by developing countries. However, the magnitude of the loss will be exaggerated if the estimate of loss is based on a price index, however weighted. Market prices relate to particular varieties or grades, not to the average return as shown by the corresponding unit values. Since market prices normally fluctuate more than unit values, in a period of falling prices the decline in unit values tends to be smaller than the fall shown in price quotations, so that the use of price indices will give an upward bias to the calculation of export volume, and thus to the terms of trade loss.

For this reason, a new series for the unit value of commodity exports from developing countries has been computed for the two decades 1970 to 1990. As expected, this new index shows a significantly smaller decline from the 1980 level than does the corresponding price index. Between 1980 and 1990, for example, the UNCTAD commodity price index fell by 26 per cent, whereas the new unit value index shows a fall of 20 per cent. Consequently, the volume increase between these two years is reduced from 65 per cent (using the price index) to 53 per cent (with the new unit value index).

The experience of the 1980s was in sharp contrast to that of the 1970s. Between the years 1970 and 1980, the volume of commodity exports and their purchasing power over manufactured imports both rose at much the same rate, so that the foreign exchange loss due to price changes was purely marginal. From 1980 to 1990, however, a great gap opened up between export volume and export purchasing power owing to the terms of trade deterioration. In the one year 1990, the resulting foreign exchange loss amounted to some \$68 billion (Table 2.2) which considerably exceeded the total of OECD aid to developing countries (of some \$50 billion) in that year.

Moreover, the foreign exchange loss had itself risen sharply since the early 1980s, from annual averages of some \$6 billion during 1981–85 to \$37 billion in 1986–88, and to \$61 billion in 1989–90. For the whole decade (1980–90), the annual average terms of trade loss was equivalent to nearly 25 per cent of the value of commodity exports in 1980; by 1989–90, the corresponding loss had more than doubled (Table 2.3). The terms of trade loss of the 1980s was also significantly greater than the equivalent experience during the Great Depression of the 1930s when the annual average terms of trade loss of the present group of developing countries over the years 1930 to 1938 amounted to some 16–17 per cent of the pre-recession (1929) level of their commodity exports.[4]

In relation to GDP, the terms of trade loss was much greater for Africa than for Asia or Latin America. This was to be expected, since the relative importance of the commodity sector is much greater in the economies of African countries than elsewhere. On a cumulative basis, the terms of trade loss for Africa (excluding Nigeria and other oil exporters) was equivalent to as much as one-quarter of aggregate GDP in 1980 – an enormous drain on

Table 2.2 Commodity exports of developing countries: 1970, 1980 and 1990

	Unit values[a]			Value of commodity exports		
	Commodities exports	Manufactures imports[b]	Commodity terms of trade[c]	At current unit value	At 1980 commodity unit value	At 1980 manufactures unit value
	(1980 = 100)				($ billion)	
1970	33	34	97	28	85	84
1980	100	100	100	109	109	109
1990	80	136	59	134	166	98
Annual average change (%)						
1970–80	11.7	11.4	0.3	14.6	2.5	2.7
1980–90	–2.2	3.1	–5.1	2.1	4.3	–1.1

Sources: As for Table 1, and author's estimates.

(a) In terms of US dollars.
(b) UN index of unit value of exports of manufactures from developed market economy countries.
(c) Unit value of commodity exports deflated by unit value of manufactures imports.

Table 2.3   Volume and price effects influencing the purchasing power of commodity exports from developing countries: 1980–90

| | 1980 | Change from 1980 (annual averages) | | |
		1981–85	1986–88	1989–90	1981–90
	($ billion)				
Volume[a]	109.0	7.4	26.4	55.0	22.6
Unit value effects:					
Exports	–	–18.0	–23.0	–30.6	–22.0
Imports[b]	–	11.6	–14.1	–30.1	–4.5
Terms of trade	–	–6.4	–37.2	–60.7	–26.5
Purchasing power					
of exports[c]	109.0	1.0	–10.8	–5.7	–3.9

Sources: *UNCTAD Commodity Yearbook*, 1992; New York, United Nations; UN Monthly Bulletin of Statistics (various issues); UN trade tapes.

(a) Value at 1980 prices.
(b) UN index of unit value exports of manufacturers from developed market-economy countries.
(c) Current value of exports deflated by UN index of unit value of exports of manufactures from developed market-economy countries (equal to volume change *minus* terms of trade effect).

resources. For Asia and Latin America, the corresponding losses were smaller, though still very substantial: 12 per cent for Asia and 14 per cent for Latin America.[5]

It is of some interest to compare these losses with the real income transfers from OECD countries as a result of the two oil 'shocks' of the 1970s. Both in 1973–4 and 1978–9, sharp increases in oil prices resulted in large real income transfers from OECD countries, equivalent in each case to about 2 per cent of their combined GDP.[6] The corresponding annual average terms of trade loss for Africa in the 1980s represented some 2.5 per cent of the region's GDP in 1980, while for Asia the proportion was about 1 per cent, and for Latin America 1.5 per cent. However, the comparison with the oil price 'shock' for the OECD countries needs to be made with two considerations in mind. First, the OECD losses during two particular short periods were largely recouped, in real terms, by subsequent increases in the prices of their manufactured exports, whereas the terms of trade losses of the commodity-dependent countries have now been prolonged for over a decade and, moreover, the rate of loss has risen very substantially in recent years. Second, these countries are also very much poorer than the OECD group (with GDP per head in 1980 only 6 per cent of the OECD average), so that even an equal percentage loss of GDP would have been a much greater disaster for the commodity-dependent countries than for the relatively wealthy member countries of OECD.

For the great majority of commodity-dependent countries, the sharp fall in commodity prices in the early 1980s and their persistently depressed levels since then, have seriously weakened their development process. For many of these countries, the adverse effects of the terms of trade losses were compounded by abnormally high interest rates on their foreign debt as well as by the virtual cessation of commercial loans. The resulting economic and social difficulties faced were also exacerbated in many developing regions, especially in Africa, by civil wars, severe and prolonged drought, and inefficient and inadequate government policies. However, the adverse change in the external economic environment would seem to have been a major underlying cause of the development crisis.

IMF stabilization 'packages' have given priority to restriction of the government's role in the economy, to monetary deflation, currency devaluation, import liberalization and increased incentives for export. One fairly general result has been to exacerbate domestic inflation and thereby to reduce real wages of employees and real incomes of peasant producers. As a result, real production costs have been reduced significantly for a range of enterprises, particularly in mining and estate agriculture. Though many such enterprises can remain profitable even at current depressed levels of world prices for their output, this by itself cannot overcome the foreign exchange crisis of the producing countries, or the budgetary problems of their governments, particularly in a period of rising import prices, reflecting continuing inflationary pressures in the industrialized countries.

To sum up: the terms of trade deterioration suffered by the commodity-dependent countries over the period since 1980 represented a greater relative shock to their economies than experienced during the 1930s – and probably for at least a century – or experienced by the OECD countries as a result of the oil 'shocks' of the

1970s.

Moreover, the terms of trade losses of the 1980s appear to have been one element – probably a major one – in the huge debt accumulation of developing countries over the decade. Between 1980 and 1990, the outstanding long-term foreign debt of developing countries (excluding major petroleum exporters, which do not have significant non-oil commodity exports) rose by some $440 billion. Though it cannot be assumed that most developing countries suffering terms of trade losses necessarily offset them by additional borrowing on international capital markets, many such countries did in fact increase their commercial borrowings or received more concessional aid from bilateral and/or multilateral sources. The cumulative terms of trade loss over the decade of some $265 billion must therefore have contributed to a significant extent to the build-up of debt, and hence to the abnormally high burden of debt service. Many commodity-dependent countries have been caught in a 'debt trap', in which the burden of debt service has forced them to expand their commodity exports,[7] which have only added to the depressive forces on world commodity prices and on their revenues from commodity exports, thus necessitating the securing of new loans and recurrent debt restructuring.

International Policy

It has been generally recognized since the mid-1980s that most heavily indebted developing countries are unlikely, on present trends in the global economy, to be able to service their foreign debts and, at the same time, to stabilize their economies and lay the basis for needed structural change and economic growth in the future. The seven large industrial countries (G-7) eventually formed a strategy to alleviate the debt burden (the 'Baker initiative' of 1985, followed by the 'Brady initiative' of 1989), which has since been extended, particularly by the introduction of more favourable terms for rescheduling official debt. Though a number of heavily indebted developing countries, many in Latin America, have reduced their debt overhang substantially as a result, the overall picture remains one of excessive debt service obligations in relation to the ability to meet those obligations as well as to finance domestic stabilization and growth.

Since ability to meet debt service obligations rests essentially on revenue from commodity exports – for the majority of developing countries – there is a strong general case for measures to raise real commodity prices from persistently depressed levels so as to complement measures to reduce the debt overhang and/or to encourage the flow of financial resources to highly-indebted commodity-dependent countries. However, the G-7 countries have been traditionally strongly opposed to any proposal for measures involving intervention in world commodity markets in order to raise prices – irrespective of whether or not those prices have been at historically low levels for many years. Various arguments have been used in support of this position, the more important ones being (i) that measures to raise commodity prices would be an inefficient means of transferring resources to developing countries compared with direct aid, and (ii) that such measures would distort commodity markets by encouraging unnecessary increases in production, thus entailing a misallocation of resources.

As regards (i), the comparison depends essentially on the meaning attached to the term 'efficiency'. If this is taken to mean the contribution made to economic development, then the efficiency of direct aid will depend on the type of aid, the conditions attached, and the use made of it by the recipient government. Equally, the efficiency of measures to raise commodity prices will depend essentially on the ability and willingness of governments to devote the additional foreign exchange to development purposes. Thus, the efficiency of such measures is likely to vary substantially among the different exporting countries, both because a given price increase will have different implications for the export revenues of different countries, and because of the different ways in which their governments deal with the increased revenues.

Moreover, aid is usually subject to restrictive conditions, both as to its use and, increasingly, as to domestic economic and political policies, which may well reduce the efficiency of aid in relation to other means of financing development. In any case, aid flows alone cannot be expected to meet more than a small proportion of the foreign exchange requirements of most commodity-dependent countries, so that aid is best considered as a supporting mechanism, rather than as a substitute, for measures to raise prices from depressed levels.

As regards the argument that measures that raise prices above market levels will inevitably result in a misallocation of resources by encouraging unnecessary increases in production, it can be pointed out that many commodity markets are already subject to major imperfections. Where there is an oligopolistic market structure, or where the market is heavily influenced by national or regional policies, decisions on investment, output and prices can diverge substantially from those that would be obtained in a perfectly competitive market. For a wide range of agricultural products, huge distortions in global resource allocation have resulted, over many years, from heavy subsidies for high-cost domestic production in all the developed countries, totalling about $300 billion a year.[8] It remains to be seen whether these subsidies will be phased out, wholly or in part, as a result of the continuing negotiations in GATT.

The depression in world commodity prices has had, by contrast, catastrophic effects on the economies of a large number of developing countries. The contraction in revenues from agricultural export crops has generally resulted in reductions in the employed labour force and in real wages, and in reductions in imported intermediates such as fertilizers and insecticides. In mining, the price fall has had adverse effects on investment and in maintenance work, with large labour reductions in small, labour-intensive mines. Moreover, government revenues – which are generally heavily dependent on export taxes or taxes on corporations involved in foreign trade – have also been adversely affected by the decline in commodity prices, and the ensuing budgetary squeeze has typically resulted in cuts in spending on human resources development, and in consequent deterioration in health, nutrition and education standards, in a large number of commodity-dependent countries.

Measures that raise current depressed prices of commodities exported wholly or mainly by developing countries by modest amounts (e.g. half-way back to the 1980 level) would thus operate to reduce the unemployed labour force, increase essential imports and maintenance work, and alleviate the squeeze on government budgets. Such measures are unlikely, by themselves, to result in a major shift of employed resources into commodity production from other sectors.

Moreover, where developing country exports are directly competitive with high-cost subsidized production in the industrial countries – as is the case, for example, for sugar, many vegetable oilseeds and oils, rice and raw cotton – a disproportionate part of the real cost of the consequent misallocation of resources falls on developing country producers, who are faced with curtailed markets and reduced prices and earnings. Measures designed to raise depressed commodity prices on world markets would, to some extent, help to redress this situation, in so far as higher prices could be considered as a form of partial compensation to developing countries for loss of export markets and export earnings brought about by the protectionist policies of industrial countries.

It is, in any case, not credible for developed country representatives to argue in international forums against possible measures to raise prices of commodities exported by developing countries on the grounds of resource misallocation in view of the widespread intervention by their own governments in their domestic markets, covering not only agriculture but also a wide range of manufacturers, such as textiles, clothing, footwear, steel and automobiles.

A more credible explanation of developed country opposition to proposals to raise depressed levels of commodity prices is that these countries greatly benefit in the short term from continuing low prices for their imports of commodities, which have played an important part in reducing their rates of inflation.[9] Moreover, measures to improve the export earnings of commodity-dependent developing countries would tend to reduce the leverage exercised by the IMF and World Bank over the domestic economic policies of these countries.[10] For both these reasons, G-7 governments are unlikely to agree to measures, such as supply management schemes, which would raise depressed levels of prices of commodities exported by developing countries.

Supply Management

A 'second best' approach for these countries would be to consider producer-only supply management approaches. However, this approach would be much more difficult to apply, other than to a limited range of commodities, than the usual kind of agreement involving both producers and consumers. This is mainly because for a large number of commodities developing countries supply only a part of the world market, while most of their industrial materials exports face competition from synthetics or other substitutes in their main end-uses. In either case, price-substitution elasticities are likely to be high. However, for the tropical beverage crops – cocoa, coffee and tea – and for certain tropical fruits, natural rubber and certain non-ferrous metals, viable supply management schemes operated by developing countries would be technically feasible. For beverage crops, especially, demand elasticities are low, while developing countries are sole (or almost sole) suppliers to the world market.

It would be important for export regulation schemes based on export quotas to have a modest price objective, and not to aim at raising prices unduly (as would a normal producers' cartel), in order for consumer interests to consider the schemes as fair and reasonable. An alternative to schemes having agreed price objectives would be intergovernmental arrangements aimed solely to reduce or eliminate a large stock 'overhang' where there is a clear structural oversupply. To the extent to which excess stocks are thereby reduced, the downward pressure on prices would be lessened or even reversed. Such arrangements should be easier to negotiate than export quota schemes, and should not evoke opposition from consumers. This was the approach used by the tin-producing countries following the collapse of the tin agreement in October 1985, with a certain degree of success.

A further alternative that might merit consideration would be the imposition of a uniform *ad valorem* export tax by all, or all the main, countries producing a particular commodity. It would, of course, be essential to cover a high proportion of available, or potentially available, supply since otherwise the importing countries could switch their purchases to producing countries not imposing the tax. One advantage of this approach is that it should be much easier to negotiate than an export quota scheme (which often involves difficult negotiations on market shares), since an export tax, being at a uniform rate, would not discriminate as between different producing countries, so that it would not affect their relative cost or relative selling prices.[11] A disadvantage of the tax approach, however, is that for commodities for which the short-term price elasticity of demand and/or supply is relatively low, a high rate of tax would be required to achieve the same percentage increase in export revenue that would be obtained by a relatively small reduction in supply.

Any of these, or other, approaches to supply management would not have been possible within the framework of the traditional type of international commodity agreement (ICA), such as those for cocoa, coffee and tin, all of which were operative at various periods over the past decade – with mixed degrees of success – in maintaining prices within agreed ranges. All three ICAs have now collapsed, essentially because of a fundamental disagreement between developing exporting countries and developed importing countries over the objectives of price stabilization. Apart from cocoa, for which a new ICA was negotiated in 1993 to include a production regulation scheme, it now seems unlikely that any other ICA will be renegotiated on this basis. For coffee, however, an export retention scheme was established, also in 1993, by producers and, if successful, may well encourage producers of other commodities in structural surplus to consider some form of supply management also.

As indicated earlier, supply management by producer interests is likely to be feasible only for a limited number of commodities. There is a considerable history of producer cooperation in the framework of the various ICAs for cocoa, coffee and natural rubber, so that it should be possible for producing countries to negotiate viable supply management schemes for these commodities. For tea, the technical conditions for a successful scheme exist, but so far there has been no agreement among producing countries for joint action. These four commodities together accounted in 1990 for $15 billion in export earnings, or almost 40 per cent of total earnings of developing countries in that year from exports of UNCTAD's 10 'core' commodities. Thus, successful supply management schemes for the tropical beverages and natural rubber would cover a substantial proportion of the value of exports of 'problem' commodities.

For most other major commodities, however, supply management would not seem to be a viable option, for reasons given earlier. Thus, a supply management approach would need to be supported by an adequate international system of low-conditionality finance to offset shortfalls of commodity export earnings below some previously agreed norm. The two existing international facilities – the IMF's Compensatory and Contingency Finance Facility, and the European Community's STABEX – have proved inadequate in relation to the need. The IMF Compensatory Finance Facility, which began in 1963 as a low-conditionality semi-automatic mechanism for temporary balance of payments support (now merged with a Contingency Facility) is now highly conditional on

IMF approval of the domestic adjustment policies of borrowing developing countries, and has operated since the mid-1980s in a pro-cyclical manner, with large net flows of financial resources to it from developing countries. The STABEX scheme has benefited very few developing countries, and is not a net addition to the aid budget of the European Community.

Diversification

Even if successful, supply management schemes would be essentially short-term expedients to alleviate the continuing foreign exchange crisis of commodity-dependent countries. In the medium and long term, many of these countries will need to diversify their economies away from specializing in the production of commodities in chronic oversupply, particularly if they are, or have become, high cost producers. Whether such diversification should be in favour of non-traditional commodities, of processing and manufacturing production, or of service industries, or some combination of these, will depend on existing and potential resource availabilities, including capital and labour skills, and on potential market outlets. Governments will need to consider these and related factors in the context of 'dynamic comparative advantage', allowing for the potential of learning-by-doing and the need to utilize appropriate technologies.

Any such diversification is unlikely to be successful without adequate financial support. Financing of individual projects is already available on a limited scale from bilateral and multilateral sources. In the later 1980s finance in the region of $1 billion a year was committed by the various international development banks for commodity-related export-oriented diversification, representing about 5 per cent of their total annual commitments. However, these loans have been concentrated on the larger, more diversified, and generally less commodity-dependent countries, partly because low-income countries have difficulties in formulating viable diversification projects. A substantial proportion of these loans has gone to projects involving production of traditional commodities, such as cocoa, coffee, rubber and palm oil.[12] These financing activities, in which the World Bank played a major role, were one element in the very substantial expansion in the exportable production of these commodities during the 1980s – and, consequently, in the downward pressure on their prices in the world market.

This reveals an underlying weakness in the country project approach used by the international development banks, since a project that appears viable for one country can result in a general fall in prices if its output adds significantly to supplies coming on the world market, in which case the export earnings of other producing countries are adversely affected. National diversification programmes should thus take into account available projections of future market trends, while there may also be scope for some form of harmonization of such programmes, initially perhaps in the context of regional or sub-regional cooperation arrangements.

There would also be some merit in a link between the financing of diversification and the possible supply management schemes mentioned earlier. To the extent that the latter succeed in raising depressed levels of commodity prices, they could make it possible for commodity-exporting countries to earmark at least some proportion of the additional export revenue for assisting the financing of longer-term diversification and structural adjustment.

A more ambitious proposal for organizing adequate external finance for development programmes has recently been proposed by Thorvald Stoltenberg, the Norwegian Foreign Minister (1989). He proposes a series of Development Contracts between individual developing countries and donors. This would involve, first, the preparation by each country of an indicative development plan in accordance with its own national priorities, to include policies for human development, poverty alleviation, improved income distribution and unemployment reduction, with the donors providing firm assurances of the external resources needed to support the plan over an agreed plan period. The second, and complementary part of the Stoltenberg proposal would be a commitment by the country concerned to apply a policy package which would provide the necessary incentives to expand domestic production, e.g. an appropriate exchange rate and structure of relative prices, and monetary and fiscal policies designed to contain inflationary pressures.

As Jayawardena (1991) comments, the Stoltenberg proposal would allow for foreign savings to be used in support of human development or basic needs goals incorporated in the plan, and this:

> would be important particularly for African countries which encounter serious difficulties in mobilizing domestic savings against the back-

ground of cutbacks in consumption sustained in the 1980s ... if the development strategy works, the domestic savings effort can be made out of incremental income as income grows. In the initial stage, however, foreign savings support is required to get the growth process going ... (and) avoid an unnecessary and potentially explosive curtailment of already depressed levels of consumption.

It is an open question, however, whether the developed countries would be prepared to establish such a system of Development Contracts in view of the large amount of additional finance likely to be required and, more importantly, the consequent reduction in the present influence of the Bretton Woods institutions on national development policies.

2.3   THE IMPACT OF COMMODITY INSTABILITY ON THE ECONOMIES OF THE DEVELOPED COUNTRIES

Since the early 1970s there has been an increased degree of interaction between the financial markets and those for primary commodities, which has exacerbated the instabilities and uncertainties in the international economic system in general.

One mechanism linking the commodity and financial markets consists of shifts of speculative funds into, and out of, those commodity markets dealing in future contracts, such as the terminal markets for cocoa, coffee, sugar, copper, rubber, lead, tin and zinc. Over the past decade, the volume of such speculative funds has grown enormously.[13] In periods of heightened uncertainty about the future movement of commodity prices, of exchange rates, or of inflation rates, very large amounts of funds can be switched, either for hedging or for speculation, from other asset markets into commodities, or *vice versa*, thus greatly accentuating the commodity price cycle.

Another link arises through the influence of the rate of interest on the volume of commodity stocks held by private traders. Abnormally high interest rates in the 1980s greatly increased the cost of holding stocks, which was an important factor, along with the slowdown in the rate of industrial growth in the developed countries, in the reduction of stocks in those countries to minimum working levels. Where such stocks had represented a substantial proportion of global stocks of particular commodities, the reduction in private sector stocks reduced the short-term price elasticity of supply, so that a given shift in the imbalance between supply and demand would have been reflected in a greater price variation than would otherwise have occurred.

There are also linkages from commodity price changes to changes in key financial variables such as exchange rates and interest rates. Perhaps the most important of such links arises as a result of large increases in commodity prices that undermine the external payments balances of developed commodity-importing countries. As Kaldor (1976, 1983) pointed out, the normal response of governments of these countries would be to introduce restrictive monetary policies, which tend to deflate the domestic economy, as well as reducing demand for imports in general. The petroleum case is the obvious example, but a similar phenomenon could arise if commodity prices were generally to rise in a future economic upswing in the main industrial countries.

Another important linkage is from commodity prices to prices of shares on the securities markets. A general rise in commodity prices causes an increase in inflationary expectations which, in turn, leads to higher interest rates to offset the expected loss in value of financial assets. The counterpart of the higher interest rate is a fall in prices of bonds and other fixed-income securities, while the fall in bond prices induces a switch of funds to bonds from shares, thus causing share prices to fall also. This sequence of events appears to have operated in the months before the stock market crash in October 1987.[14] Thus, instability in the commodity markets and in the financial markets feed on each other, and constitute an inbuilt mechanism of short-term destabilization and uncertainty in the world economy.

Because of the low short-term price elasticities of both supply and demand for the great majority of primary commodities, any given disturbance in economic activity in the developed countries, or in commodity supply, results in a greater than proportionate change in commodity prices and in the export earnings of commodity-dependent countries. The consequent contraction in these export earnings during an economic recession then results in an adverse 'feedback' effect on the export sector of developed countries as the commodity-dependent countries perforce have to reduce their purchases of manufactured goods.

This, in turn, reinforces the original recessionary forces in the developed countries.

This appears to have been the mechanism by which the financial crisis of 1929 was turned into the Great Depression of the 1930s, as was shown by Lewis (1949). A very similar mechanism appears to have been in operation in the 1980s and early 1990s. The consequent need for a system of buffer stocks that could act as a counter-cyclical mechanism was clearly seen by Keynes (1938), and further elaborated in his wartime proposals (1942). These proposals included not only the establishment of a series of buffer stocks for the main traded commodities, but also a link between the financing of the stocks and Keynes' own suggested International Clearing Union (the latter being a blueprint for what emerged as the IMF). The General Council coordinating the various buffer stocks would hold an increasing credit balance with the Clearing Union in times of general boom when the buffer stocks were being depleted, and an increasing debit balance in times of general slump when the buffer stocks were accumulating. This would, Keynes emphasized, introduce a stabilizing factor of major importance into the world economy.

A more complex proposal, with the same objective, was made by Hart *et al.* (1964). This envisaged the creation by the IMF of a new currency (bancor), convertible into both gold and a fixed bundle of 30 or so principal commodities. By the purchase of units of the composite bundle of commodities when supply tended to outrun demand, and by the sale of these composite units in the reverse situation, this scheme would ensure that the average price of the bundle would be stabilized (in terms of bancor or gold). Moreover, the scheme would operate, in effect, as a world income-stabilizing mechanism. This proposal attracted much academic criticism and, like the Keynes proposal, was never seriously considered at the intergovernmental level. None the less, the need to create a viable international stabilizing mechanism for the world economy remains an urgent one, in the interests of both developing and developed countries.

2.4 CONCLUSIONS

This paper has argued that two key issues related to the 'commodity problem' need reappraisal. The first is the widespread view that this problem is predominantly one of short-term price instability, while acknowledging the related issue of deteriorating long-term trend in real commodity prices. The statistical evidence shows, on the other hand, that since the early 1980s the predominant feature of the commodity markets has been the persistence of abnormally depressed levels of real commodity prices, which have resulted in huge foreign exchange losses for developing countries, and associated accumulation of foreign debt and, for very many commodity-dependent countries, a sharp reduction in living standards and in domestic investment. The short-term instability problem has also remained acute for a number of important commodities.

It follows that international concern in the commodities field should now be widened from the negotiation, or renegotiation, of traditional-type ICAs designed to even out short-term price fluctuations to measures to alleviate the adverse impact of persistently depressed commodity prices on the development process. This paper has mentioned a number of possible measures that could be taken to this end.

The second issue considered above is the impact of commodity market instability, and of a deterioration in the trend of real commodity prices, on the economies of developed countries. There would appear to be several *a priori* arguments in favour of the view that commodity instability and deteriorating trend would both have adverse impacts on developed country economies.

Further empirical research on both these issues would seem to be needed. For example, as regards the first issue, it would be useful to undertake feasibility studies of alternative supply management schemes for the tropical beverages, and for natural rubber, so as to demonstrate the potential benefits and costs involved. Another relevant research theme would be the impact of the terms of trade losses suffered by commodity-dependent countries on their foreign debt since 1980, on which country case studies would be useful.

On the second issue, an analysis of the impact of commodity price instability on instability of the economies of each main developed country (distinguishing prices, wages, output, interest rates, balances of payments, etc) would be necessary in order to demonstrate the qualitative conclusions advanced in the present paper. Another useful study could relate to the 'feedback' impact on output and employment in developed countries of the deterioration since 1980 in the real prices of commodities exported by developing countries.

NOTES

1. In this paper, 'commodities' relate to raw and processed products of the primary sector (agriculture, forestry, fishing and mining), excluding petroleum.
2. See, for example, Spraos (1983), Sapsford (1985) and Sarkar (1986).
3. The World Bank (1991) envisages a decline in average real commodity prices of 5 per cent between 1991 and 1993, followed by a rise of some 10 per cent up to 2000, when the index would still be 8 per cent below the 1986–90 average.
4. See Maizels (1992), Table A.1.
5. These estimates for Asia and Latin America exclude major exporters of petroleum and major exporters of manufactures.
6. See OECD (1980).
7. See Gilbert (1989).
8. OECD (1991, a, b).
9. Beckerman (1985), and Beckerman and Jenkinson (1986).
10. According to Helleiner (1988): 'The current Washington obsession with conditionality on resource flows to the developing countries has stood the old "trade not aid" slogans on their heads. Officials in both the US government and the international financial institutions can be heard complaining that the increased price of coffee allows some countries to evade "sound" economic policies.'
11. However, the impact on the export revenues of different producing countries could vary considerably if they faced different price-elasticities of demand and/or if their short-term supply elasticities differed significantly.
12. Details of financial commitments by the World Bank and the regional Development Banks for export-orientated diversification in the commodity sector during the 1980's are given in UNCTAD (1990).
13. A broad indicator of the growth in speculation is the net size of the Eurocurrency market, which grew from $65 billion in 1970 to $1,450 billion in 1986, with further growth since then.
14. For further discussion see Avramović (1992).

REFERENCES

Avramović, D. (1992): 'Commodity problem, poor countries and poor people', Background Paper prepared for UNDP Human Development Report, 1992 (mimeo).

Beckerman, W. (1985): 'How the battle against the inflation was really won', *Lloyds Bank Review* (Jan.), 1–12.

Beckerman, W. and T. Jenkinson (1986): 'What stopped the inflation?: unemployment or commodity prices?', *Economic Journal*, **96** (Mar.), 39–54.

Gilbert, C.L. (1989): 'The impact of exchange rates and developing country debt on commodity prices', *Economic Journal*, **99** (Sept.), 773–84.

Grilli, E.R. and M.C. Yang (1988): 'Primary commodity prices, manufactured goods prices, and the terms of trade of developing countries: what the long run shows', *World Bank Economic Review*, **2** (1) (Jan.), 1–47.

Hart, A.G., N. Kaldor and J. Tinbergen (1964): 'The case for an international commodity reserve currency', in UNCTAD (1964, vol iii).

Helleiner, G.K. (1988): 'Primary commodity markets: recent trends and research requirements', in Eliot and Williamson (eds), *World Economic Problems*, Special Report 7 (July) (Washington, DC: Institute for International Economics).

Jayawardena, L. (1991): *A Global Environmental Compact for Sustainable Development: Resource Requirements and Mechanisms*, Helsinki: World Institute for Development Economics Research (UN University).

Kaldor, N. (1976): 'Inflation and recession in the world economy', *Economic Journal*, **86** (Dec.), 703–14.

—— (1983): 'The role of commodity prices in economic recovery', *Lloyds Bank Review* (July), 21–34 [reprinted in *World Development*, **15** (5) (1987), 551–8].

Keynes, J.M. (1938): 'The policy of government storage of food-stuffs and raw materials', *Economic Journal*, **48** (Sept.), 449–60.

—— (1942): 'The international regulation of primary products', reprinted in D. Moggridge (ed.) (1980): *Collected Writings of John Maynard Keynes*, **27**, London: Macmillan and Cambridge University Press, 135–66.

Lewis, W.A. (1949): *Economic Survey: 1919–1939,* (London: Allen & Unwin).

Maizels, A. (1992): *Commodities in Crisis,* (Oxford: Clarendon Press).

OECD (1980): *Economic Outlook*, **27** (July), (Paris).

—— (1991a): *Agricultural Policies, Markets and Trade: Monitoring and Outlook*, (Paris).

—— (1991b): *Development Co-operation*, (Paris).

Prebisch, R. (1950): *The Economic Development of Latin America and its Principal Problems*, (New York: United Nations).

Sapsford, D. (1985): 'The statistical debate on the net barter terms of trade between primary commodities and manufactures: a comment and some additional evidence', *Economic Journal*, **95**, 781–8.

Sarkar, P. (1986): 'The Singer–Prebisch hypothesis: a statistical evaluation', *Cambridge Journal of Economics*, **10**, 355–71.

Singer, H.W. (1950): 'The distribution of gains between investing and borrowing countries', *American Economic Review*, **40** (May), 473–85.

Spraos, J. (1983): *Inequalizing Trade?*, (Oxford: Clarendon Press).

Stoltenberg, T. (1989): 'Towards a world development strategy based on growth, sustainability and solidarity: policy options for the 1990s', paper presented at OECD Development Centre 25th Anniversary Symposium, (Paris) (Feb.).

UNCTAD (1964): *Proceedings of the United Nations Conference on Trade and Development*, (New York UN).

—— (1990): *Financial Resources for Diversification Projects and Programmes*, (17 Aug.).

World Bank (1991): *Price Prospects for Major Primary Commodities*, (Washington, DC).

3. The Excess Co-movement of Commodity Prices Revisited*

S. J. Leybourne, T. A. Lloyd and G. V. Reed

3.1 INTRODUCTION

It is observed empirically that the prices of internationally traded commodities have a tendency to move together (co-move) over time. Indeed, it is common for commodity market traders and brokers to ascribe the increase in the price of one commodity to the fact that other commodity prices have risen. Clearly, price co-movement of commodities that are either substitutes or complements in consumption and/or production is not surprising. In a similar vein, the prices of unrelated commodities (that is to say commodities for which cross-price elasticities of demand and supply are close to zero) may also co-move owing to the effects of macroeconomic factors such as aggregate demand, inflation and exchange and interest rates that are common determinants of all commodity prices. For example, an increase in the rate of industrial production will bolster the demand for industrial commodities that are used as inputs into production, such as crude oil, copper and lumber. The resultant higher income will in turn raise the demand for non-industrial commodities such as wheat and coffee. Such effects generate co-movement in commodity prices, which, it should be stressed, are nominal and not real. Alogoskoufis *et al.* (1990) contend that much of the commodity price upswing in the 1970s was due to the low interest rates that accompanied the

*An earlier version of this paper was presented at the 'Commodities Conference' hosted jointly by CREDIT University of Nottingham and the Department of Economics, University of Lancaster, held at Ambleside, Cumbria, 24–26 May 1993. We would like to thank all those present for their comments, particularly Christopher Gilbert and the editors of this volume.

expansionary policies in industrial countries, and that the downturn witnessed in the 1980s reflected the tightening of monetary and fiscal policies during that period.

In a recent paper, Pindyck and Rotemberg (1990) (henceforth PR), examine this issue and find that, even after accounting for the effects of macroeconomic influences, the prices of unrelated commodities still exhibit significant co-movement. They have called this phenomenon *excess co-movement*. It is of interest to economists since it represents a rejection of the standard model of competitive commodity price formation with storage, possibly (although not necessarily) implying an element of irrational behaviour in what are typically regarded as some of the most highly competitive markets in the world.

Excess co-movement is principally attributed to two sources: 'herd' behaviour and liquidity effects. Herd behaviour (or sympathetic speculative buying) arises if traders interpret 'news' in a similar way across all commodities for little or no apparent reason. Traders are thus alternatively bullish or bearish in all commodity markets without economic justification, their behaviour merely reflecting some subjective consensus of confidence or timidity. Such behaviour is believed to underlie the temporary rise of most commodity prices at the outbreak of the Gulf War. Alternatively, traders may require time to decipher the implications of certain news, and thus react in a similar way across all commodities, only later making adjustments that reflect the commodity-specific implications of the original news. Compounding the herd effect is the use of automated trading strategies that embody simple decision rules based on rates of change of prices. Market temperament and the adoption of automated trading strategies may imply irrationality, but are used by commodity traders as heuristic devices in the presence of a vast and continual information flow. It is also suggested that liquidity constraints link the prices of unrelated commodities, in that a fall in the price of one commodity causes other commodity prices to fall because it reduces the liquidity of speculators who are 'long' in several commodities at once. In other words, those speculators who are caught holding commodity futures purchased at a high price may, when spot prices are lower and falling, be expected to sell futures in other commodities to cover margin calls (the difference between spot and agreed futures prices) in the commodity in which they are long.

Despite the apparent plausibility of such effects, recent evidence proposed by Palakas and Varangis (1991), (henceforth PV) casts some doubt on the findings of PR, in that excess co-movement is found to be the exception rather than the rule across the prices of unrelated commodities.

This paper formalizes a framework for the testing of the excess co-movement hypothesis. This paper is purely methodological: we make no attempt to test empirically the hypothesis of excess co-movement, preferring to identify methodological problems in previous work and establish a tractable framework for further research. The paper begins, in Section 3.2, with a brief review of the previous approaches employed to detect excess co-movement and the problems encountered. As we illustrate in Section 3.3, excess co-movement is a phenomenon with a somewhat richer structure than was previously acknowledged. In that section of the paper we provide simple definitions of co-movement and excess co-movement in terms of their time series properties and thus derive a testing framework. While two approaches have been developed to test the hypothesis empirically, little attention has been paid to methodological issues, and as we demonstrate in Section 3.4 this oversight leads, in one case, to deficient tests and misleading results. In that section we use Monte Carlo simulation to estimate the powers of our proposed test for excess co-movement and that of the other methodologically acceptable approach. Section 3.5 offers some concluding comments.

3.2 PREVIOUS APPROACHES

There have been two attempts to test the hypothesis of excess co-movement. The first of these, by PR, is based on a standard competitive model of commodity price formation with storage, from which commodity price equations are then derived. The second, a response to the PR paper, is due to PV. A brief description of these approaches is given below.

We use the following definitions throughout:

$P_{i,t}$ – the (logarithm) of the price of commodity i in period t, $i = 1, ..., n$,

$X_{j,t}$ – the (logarithm) of macroeconomic variable j in period t, $j = 1, ..., m$.

$\varepsilon_{j,t}$ – a random disturbance in the ith equation in period t, with mean zero, $t = 1, ..., T$.

The Pindyck and Rotemberg Approach

PR use the following commodity price equation as the basis for their test for excess co-movement:

$$\Delta P_{i,t} = \sum_{k=0}^{K} \alpha'_{i,k} \Delta X_{t-k} + \varepsilon_{i,t} \tag{3.1}$$

where $\alpha_{i,k}$ is an $m \times 1$ vector of parameters and X_t is the $m \times 1$ vector of macroeconomic variables. PR hypothesize that excess co-movement between prices $P_{i,t}$ and $P_{j,t}$ manifests itself as a non-zero contemporaneous correlation between $\varepsilon_{i,t}$ and $\varepsilon_{j,t}$, on the assumption that all relevant macroeconomic variables have been included in Equation 3.1. Their tests of the null hypothesis of no excess co-movement are based on the contemporaneous correlations of the disturbances. They estimate the residuals from the commodity price equations, both in unrestricted form and under the restriction that the contemporaneous correlation matrix is diagonal, and then test whether each pair of disturbances is correlated and whether the disturbance correlation matrix for all disturbances is diagonal. The latter test is performed using a likelihood-ratio statistic with an asymptotic χ^2 distribution. They find that 5 of the 21 possible pairings of disturbances from the 7 commodity prices considered are significantly correlated at the 5 per cent level. Their diagonality test rejects the null hypothesis at the 1 per cent level.

PR acknowledge that Equation 3.1 may be under-parameterised because individuals may have access to information that lies outside *any set* of past and current observable macroeconomic variables. Qualitative information, by definition, is difficult to incorporate in time series regression, yet could in principle affect all commodity prices and thus account for the apparent excess co-movement. To circumvent the need to incorporate 'the unmeasurable' directly, PR augment Equation 3.1 with *latent variables*, which represent 'the market's forecasts of future values of the macroeconomic variables' (p.1182), and should, they suggest, embody the qualitative information that might be driving commodity prices. Inclusion of two latent variables (representing current forecasts of next period's rate of industrial production and inflation) slightly improves the explanatory power of the commodity price regressions; however, there is still evidence of excess co-movement at the 1 per cent level.

In concluding their analysis, PR suggest three potential problems that may account for the apparent presence of excess co-movement, namely the endogeneity of the macroeconomic variables, non-normality of commodity price distributions, and missing variables. Of the latter they state: 'Indeed, a major limitation of our approach is that we can never be sure we have included all relevant macroeconomic variables and latent variables' (p. 1185). This is an important *caveat* to which we shall return in Section 3.3.

The Palaskas and Varangis Approach

PV focus on the time series properties of commodity prices and utilise the isomorphism between co-integration and error correction mechanisms (see Engle and Granger, 1987) as a basis for testing the excess co-movement hypothesis.

The testing procedure begins with an evaluation of the time series properties of the series of interest; namely a set of commodity prices and a group of macroeconomic variables similar to those used by PR. Specifically, they assume that all the commodity prices and macroeconomic variables are generated by a process that is integrated of order one I (1), i.e. they all may be represented in a generic fashion as:

$$Z_t = Z_{t-1} + e_t$$

where e_t is a stationary (i.e. I(0)) process.

Following Engle and Granger (1987), a pair of I(1) commodity prices $P_{i,t}$ and $P_{j,t}$ are said to be co-integrated with parameter α if:

$$r_t = P_{i,t} - \alpha P_{j,t} \tag{3.2}$$

is a stationary process. Granger's Representation Theorem (see Engle and Granger, 1987) proves the general result that if two series co-integrate then there must exist an error correction mechanism (ECM) linking the series, having the form:

$$\Delta P_{i,t} = \gamma r_{t-1} + \kappa \Delta P_{j,t} + \eta_{i,t} \tag{3.3}$$

where $\eta_{i,t}$ is a stationary process.

PV augment Equation 3.3 by including current (and if necessary lagged) values of the macroeconomic variables, giving:

$$\Delta P_{i,t} = \gamma r_{t-1} + \kappa \Delta P_{j,t} + \zeta' \Delta X_t + \eta_{i,t} \qquad (3.4)$$

More generally, lagged values of the two price series are also included as regressors to account for any serial correlation in $\eta_{i,t}$ but are omitted here for simplicity.

Their approach to examining excess co-movement begins by assuming that if $P_{i,t}$ and $P_{j,t}$ draw on a common information set of I(1) macroeconomic variables, as co-integration requires, and that $\Delta P_{j,t}$ significantly explains $\Delta P_{i,t}$ then, they argue that the explanatory power of $\Delta P_{j,t}$ can be proxied by changes in those common macroeconomic variables. In terms of Equation 3.4, where ΔX_t is included, they suggest that the OLS estimate of κ should become insignificant. Hence, they define excess co-movement as the case where the estimate of κ remains significant in the presence of ΔX_t owing to their belief that in some sense this measures the correlation between prices above and beyond that which can be accounted for by the common set of macroeconomic variables.

The hypothesis $\kappa = 0$ is tested using the ratio of the likelihoods from the unrestricted ECM, (Equation 3.4), and the restricted ECM given by setting $\kappa = 0$ in Equation 3.4. Broadly speaking they find that out of the 21 pairs of commodity prices tested only 4 reject the null hypothesis of no excess co-movement at the 5 per cent level using annual data and 7 out of the 21 pairs reject the null with monthly data. However, PV point out that the distribution of the statistic they use to test the null hypothesis is reliant upon normality of the regression residuals, and this assumption is violated in all the monthly regressions and in all but the regressions for the coffee–cocoa pairing with annual data. They attribute excess co-movement in this case to the effect of common weather shocks, given that these crops are grown in similar regions of the world. Hence, they find little reliable evidence supporting the hypothesis of excess co-movement amongst *unrelated* commodity prices. Where evidence of excess co-movement is found it is inconclusive owing to the size distortion of their tests caused by non-normality.

In summary, the two approaches discussed here offer contradictory conclusions: whereas PR's study suggest that excess co-movement in unrelated commodity prices occurs quite generally, PV conclude that it is very much the exception to the rule. With this in mind we proceed to a more detailed evaluation of the two approaches.

3.3 A CONCEPTUAL FRAMEWORK FOR IDENTIFYING EXCESS CO-MOVEMENT

In this section we consider the following simple model as a vehicle in which we can embed the previous approaches, identifying their weakness in both conception and practice, and also develop our proposed methodology. Let:

$$P_{1,t} = \alpha_1 X_{1,t} + \alpha_2 X_{2,t} + v_{1,t} \qquad (3.5)$$

$$P_{2,t} = \beta_1 X_{1,t} + \beta_2 X_{2,t} + v_{2,t} \qquad (3.6)$$

with

$$v_{1,t} = \alpha_3 N_t + \varepsilon_{1,t}$$

$$v_{2,t} = \beta_3 N_t + \varepsilon_{2,t}$$

where $P_{1,t}$ and $P_{2,t}$ are the prices of two commodities, $X_{1,t}$ and $X_{2,t}$ are two macroeconomic variables and $\varepsilon_{1,t}$ and $\varepsilon_{2,t}$ represent two independent I(0) disturbance terms. Here, N_t denotes an unobserved I(0) 'news' variable that incorporates information that is possibly common to both prices, and is readily identified as the source of possible excess co-movement when α_3 and β_3 are both non-zero and of the same sign. Note that N_t cannot be an I(1) variable, for reasons that will shortly become apparent. In keeping with the previous approaches we assume that all prices and macroeconomic variables follow I(1) processes. We consider first the approach adopted by PR.

Pindyck and Rotemberg

Case 1: model correctly specified
PR would estimate:

$$\Delta P_{1,t} = \alpha_1 \Delta X_{1,t} + \alpha_2 \Delta X_{2,t} + u_{1,t}$$

$$\Delta P_{2,t} = \beta_1 \Delta X_{1,t} + \beta_2 \Delta X_{2,t} + u_{2,t}$$

so that

$$u_{1,t} = \Delta v_{1,t} = \alpha_3 \Delta N_t + \Delta \varepsilon_{1,t}$$
$$u_{2,t} = \Delta v_{2,t} = \beta_3 \Delta N_t + \Delta \varepsilon_{2,t}$$

Their test for excess co-movement is based on the correlation of the residuals $\hat{u}_{1,t}$ and $\hat{u}_{2,t}$, and in this case their procedure should correctly identify the presence of the common news variable.

Case 2: model incorrectly specified

Suppose that the macroeconomic variable $X_{2,t}$ is omitted, so that the estimated equations are now

$$\Delta P_{1,t} = \alpha_1 \Delta X_{1,t} + u_{1,t}$$
$$\Delta P_{2,t} = \beta_1 \Delta X_{1,t} + u_{2,t}$$

where

$$u_{1,t} = \alpha_2 \Delta X_{2,t} + \alpha_3 \Delta N_t + \Delta \varepsilon_{1,t}$$
$$u_{2,t} = \beta_2 \Delta X_{2,t} + \beta_3 \Delta N_t + \Delta \varepsilon_{2,t}$$

Now $\hat{u}_{1,t}$ and $\hat{u}_{2,t}$ will be correlated, even when α_3 or β_3 (or both) equal zero, so that excess co-movement would apparently exist. This is wholly due to the omission of the macroeconomic variable $\Delta X_{2,t}$ whose effect is now expressed in the error term. Clearly such excess co-movement would be entirely spurious. If both α_3 and β_3 are non-zero then excess co-movement should be detected, but the genuine news-based correlation would be confounded by the effect of the omitted macroeconomic variable.

Palaskas and Varangis

We now consider the PV approach. As we shall show, their method does not permit a valid test for excess co-movement, so that we need not distinguish between the two separate cases considered above. The first stage in their analysis requires that $P_{1,t}$ and $P_{2,t}$ co-integrate. Assume that the model specified in Equations 3.5 and 3.6 holds. Then $P_{1,t}$ and $P_{2,t}$ will co-integrate only if the coefficients of the I(1) macroeconomic variables obey the restrictions

$$\alpha_1 = \pi \beta_1$$

$$\alpha_2 = \pi\beta_2$$

for some non-zero π. In this case, the error correction model relating the two prices may be written as

$$\Delta P_{1,t} = \pi\Delta P_{2,t} - (P_{1,t-1} - \pi P_{2,t-1}) + w_t$$

where

$$w_t = v_{1,t} - \pi v_{2,t} = (\alpha_3 - \pi\beta_3)N_t + \varepsilon_{1,t} - \pi\varepsilon_{2,t}$$

Note that if the news variable were I(1) then the two prices would only co-integrate if the parameters on the news variable obeyed the same restriction as that on the parameters of the macroeconomic variables, that is $\alpha_3 = \pi\beta_3$.

If the prices co-integrate, PV would estimate the augmented model

$$\Delta P_{1,t} = \pi\Delta P_{2,t} - (P_{1,t-1} - \pi P_{2,t-1}) + \delta_1\Delta X_{1,t} + \delta_2\Delta X_{2,t} + w_t \quad (3.7)$$

and perform a likelihood ratio test of $\pi = 0$. They argue that rejection of this null indicates the presence of excess co-movement, the basis being the presumption that $\Delta P_{2,t}$ would embody information not present in the macroeconomic variables; this additional information corresponds, in our terminology, to the 'news' variable. While this approach has superficial intuitive appeal it ignores the fact that the effect of the common news variable shows up in the error term

$$w_t = (\alpha_3 - \pi\beta_3)N_t + \varepsilon_{1,t} - \pi\varepsilon_{2,t}$$

(for $\alpha_3 - \pi\beta_3 \neq 0$) rather than in the coefficient of $\Delta P_{2,t}$ being driven to zero. They appear to believe that the test of the null $\pi = 0$ is equivalent to a test of the null that one or both of α_3 and β_3 is equal to zero, against the alternative that both are non-zero. However, it is not clear that inclusion of the $\Delta X_t s$ should imply a zero value of π, whatever the values of α_3 and β_3. To appreciate this, consider the following simplified example of Equations 3.5 and 3.6 in which there is no excess co-movement (i.e. $\alpha_3 = \beta_3 = 0$) and only one macroeconomic variable (i.e. $\alpha_2 = \beta_2 = 0$), and where without loss of generality we have set $\beta_1 = 1$, so that

$$P_{1,t} = \alpha_1 X_{1,t} + \varepsilon_{1,t} \quad (3.8)$$

$$P_{2,t} = X_{1,t} + \varepsilon_{2,t} \quad (3.9)$$

where

$$X_{1,t} = X_{1,t-1} + \eta_t \tag{3.10}$$

$P_{1,t}$ and $P_{2,t}$ will co-integrate with parameter α. We denote the OLS estimate of this parameter as $\tilde{\alpha}$. The above model has an ECM of the form

$$\Delta P_{1,t} = \alpha \Delta P_{2,t} - (P_{1,t-1} - \alpha P_{2,t-1}) + (\varepsilon_{1,t} - \alpha \varepsilon_{2,t})$$

PV would augment this model by the inclusion of $\Delta X_{1,t}$ and would estimate a model of the form

$$\Delta P_{1,t} = \alpha^* \Delta P_{2,t} - (P_{1,t-1} - \tilde{\alpha} P_{2,t-1}) + \beta^* \Delta X_{1,t} + \varepsilon_t^* \tag{3.11}$$

by OLS. They would use the estimate of α^*, $\hat{\alpha}^*$, to test the null that $\alpha = 0$. However, as we show in the Appendix, the OLS estimate of α^* tends asymptotically to a non-zero value. Their procedure is thus biased towards the rejection of the null hypothesis of no excess co-movement even when none exists in a correctly specified model. As a consequence we shall give their procedure no further consideration.[1]

A Unified Approach

It is our contention that the absence of a formal definition of excess co-movement has obstructed understanding of the phenomenon, which, we maintain, has a deeper structure than previously acknowledged. In the cited papers definitions of co-movement and excess co-movement are vague and we would suggest that this definitional imprecision has led to confusion at the testing stage. For example, it is unclear from PR whether there must exist co-movement in order to identify excess co-movement. In other words, is co-movement a necessary precursor to excess co-movement? This question raises more than mere semantics. If the answer is 'no', then estimation in first differences is 'best practice' since, providing all relevant macroeconomic variables are included, it avoids the spurious regression problem and involves no loss of information. If the answer to that question is 'yes' (and one could easily interpret this from their paper) then their equations will be mis-specified since there is no recognition of this co-movement in their estimating equations. PV explicitly confine excess co-movement to those prices that co-move in the sense that they co-integrate, but as a result exclude potentially important cases.

Specifically, excess co-movement is only of economic interest if it represents correlation of commodity prices *over and above* that which can be explained by the effect of macroeconomic variables, since this might imply that commodity traders respond systematically to information of a 'non-economic' nature. Providing all relevant macroeconomic influences have been accounted for in price regressions, excess co-movement is easily detected by the presence of correlation between residuals from these equations. It should be apparent however, from the discussion in Section 3.2, that excess co-movement may also occur from the omission of important macroeconomic variables from the price equations. In such circumstances 'excess co-movement' is little more than a trivial artefact of econometric mis-specification and thus may be termed *spurious excess co-movement*. Thus, only where *all relevant macroeconomic* variables have been specified does the presence of excess co-movement merit economic interest.

Co-integration provides a natural approach to the definition of co-movement. Consider again the simple model used in our discussion of the PV approach.

$$P_{1,t} = \alpha_1 X_{1,t} + \alpha_2 X_{2,t} + v_{1,t} \tag{3.5}$$

$$P_{2,t} = \beta_1 X_{1,t} + \beta_2 X_{2,t} + v_{2,t} \tag{3.6}$$

The two prices will only co-integrate if the parameters on the common set of macroeconomic variables obey the restrictions

$$\alpha_1 = \pi\beta_1$$

$$\alpha_2 = \pi\beta_2$$

that is, they differ only by a factor of proportionality. These requirements mean that, *inter alia*, sign (α_1/α_2) = sign (β_1/β_2). The intuition of co-movement between commodity prices suggests that we should impose a further restriction: that sign $(\partial P_1/\partial X_1)$ = sign $(\partial P_2/\partial X_1)$, so that changes in any common macroeconomic variable drive the two prices in the same direction.[2] It follows that co-integration is a necessary but not a sufficient condition for co-movement. It is of interest that PV seem prepared to accept co-integration as both a necessary and sufficient condition for co-movement. For example, they would not be concerned by two price series that diverged over time, provided that they co-integrated. We propose to use the stronger definition, that co-movement between a pair of prices exists if there is co-integration *and* the partial derivatives of the prices with respect to each macroeconomic variable have the same sign.

We then define two types of (non-spurious) excess co-movement: *strong excess co-movement* and *weak excess co-movement*. This distinction arises owing to the semantic association between co-movement and excess co-movement that is implicit in previous research. As a term, excess co-movement is unfortunate in that it implies the existence of *co-movement* against which it may somehow be assessed. It is not clear that this need be so: in essence, the presence of co-movement between two raw commodity prices is not a prerequisite for the existence of a significant correlation between the residuals from correctly specified price equations. In other words, in our terminology, co-movement refers to a common 'long-run' relationship between two prices that is I(1), whereas excess co-movement refers to correlation between the I(0) disturbances to the two prices. Our preferred terminology is that there is excess co-movement when the residuals from correctly specified price equations are correlated, but that it is *weak excess co-movement* when the raw commodity prices do not co-move, and *strong excess co-movement* when the raw commodity prices do co-move.

To clarify these definitions we shall employ three simple models in which $P_{1,t}$ and $P_{2,t}$ are two I(1) commodity prices, $X_{1,t}$ and $X_{2,t}$ are the full set of I(1) macroeconomic variables common to both prices and $\varepsilon_{1,t}$ and $\varepsilon_{2,t}$ are mutually independent random disturbance terms, therefore containing no common 'news'. Consider first

$$P_{1,t} = X_{1,t} + 2X_{2,t} + v_{1,t} \qquad (3.7)$$

$$P_{2,t} = -X_{1,t} + X_{2,t} + v_{2,t} \qquad (3.8)$$

where

$$v_{1,t} = \alpha_3 N_t + \varepsilon_{1,t}$$

$$v_{2,t} = \beta_3 N_t + \varepsilon_{2,t}$$

Although both prices have the same macroeconomic variables in common, they do not co-integrate, and so the prices do not co-move (and indeed would tend to diverge over time). There will be *weak* excess co-movement if $\alpha_3 \neq 0$ and $\beta_3 \neq 0$, no excess co-movement otherwise. The same conclusion would apply if one of the macroeconomic variables were excluded from one of the price equations.

Consider next the model

$$P_{1,t} = X_{1,t} + 2X_{2,t} + v_{1,t} \tag{3.9}$$

$$P_{2,t} = X_{1,t} - 2X_{2,t} + v_{2,t} \tag{3.10}$$

where $v_{1,t}$ and $v_{2,t}$ are defined as before. The prices will co-integrate, but since the partial derivatives of $P_{1,t}$ and $P_{2,t}$ with respect to $X_{1,t}$ have opposite signs, there is again no co-movement. There will be *weak* excess co-movement if $\alpha_3 \neq 0$ and $\beta_3 \neq 0$, no excess co-movement otherwise.

In the model

$$P_{1,t} = X_{1,t} + 2X_{2,t} + v_{1,t} \tag{3.11}$$
$$P_{2,t} = 2X_{1,t} + 4X_{2,t} + v_{2,t} \tag{3.12}$$

where $v_{1,t}$ and $v_{2,t}$ are defined as before, the prices co-integrate and the partial derivatives of $P_{1,t}$ and $P_{2,t}$ with respect to $X_{1,t}$ have the same sign, so that there is co-movement. There will be *strong* excess co-movement if $\alpha_3 \neq 0$ and $\beta_3 \neq 0$, no excess co-movement otherwise.

The PR approach cannot identify co-movement, and so can only identify weak excess co-movement. Our preferred approach allows us to distinguish between strong and weak excess co-movement, and has the added advantage of providing a means of checking that the set of macroeconomic variables is correctly specified.

3.4 COMPARING THE POWER OF THE TWO APPROACHES

The PR approach overlaps with ours in that in any case where our procedure identifies excess co-movement, whether weak or strong, the former should identify weak excess co-movement. It is therefore appropriate to consider the relative power of the two approaches. We have conducted a limited number of Monte Carlo experiments in which stylized versions of both approaches are applied using the following data-generation process.

$$P_{1,t} = X_{1,t} + X_{2,t} + v_{1,t} \tag{3.13}$$

$$P_{2,t} = X_{1,t} + X_{2,t} + v_{2,t} \qquad (3.14)$$

where

$$X_{1,t} = X_{1,t-1} + \eta_{1,t} \qquad (3.15)$$

$$X_{2,t} = X_{2,t-1} + \eta_{2,t} \qquad (3.16)$$

with $\eta_{1,t} \sim nid\ (0,1)$, $\eta_{2,t} \sim nid\ (0,1)$.[3] The disturbances in the two price equations are generated as

$$v_{1,t} = N_t + \varepsilon_{1,t} \qquad (3.17)$$

$$v_{2,t} = N_t + \varepsilon_{2,t} \qquad (3.18)$$

with $\varepsilon_{1,t} \sim nid\ (0,1)$, $\varepsilon_{2,t} \sim nid\ (0,1)$, and with $N_t \sim nid\ (0,\sigma_N^2)$. All the disturbances are also mutually independent.

To implement the PR approach in this simple model we first assume that both $X_{1,t}$ and $X_{2,t}$ are (correctly) included in the set of macroeconomic variables, and perform the following regressions.

$$\Delta P_{1,t} = \hat{\alpha}_1 \Delta X_{1,t} + \hat{\alpha}_2 \Delta X_{2,t} + \hat{u}_{1,t} \qquad (3.19)$$

$$\Delta P_{2,t} = \hat{\beta}_1 \Delta X_{1,t} + \hat{\beta}_2 \Delta X_{2,t} + \hat{u}_{2,t} \qquad (3.20)$$

The correlation between the disturbances is estimated from the regression of $\hat{u}_{1,t}$ on $\hat{u}_{2,t}$. Under the null hypothesis of zero excess co-movement (i.e. that $\sigma_N^2 = 0$) the corresponding t-ratio is asymptotically distributed as $N(0,1)$ since all variables are I(0).

Our proposed approach proceeds by estimating the regressions

$$P_{1,t} = \hat{\alpha}_1 X_{1,t} + \hat{\alpha}_2 X_{2,t} + \hat{v}_{1,t} \qquad (3.21)$$

$$P_{2,t} = \hat{\beta}_1 X_{1,t} + \hat{\beta}_2 X_{2,t} + \hat{v}_{2,t} \qquad (3.22)$$

Since Equations 3.21 and 3.22 represent co-integrating regressions the residuals $\hat{v}_{1,t}$ and $\hat{v}_{2,t}$ are I(0). We then estimate the correlation between the disturbances from the regression of $\hat{u}_{1,t}$ on $\hat{u}_{2,t}$. Again, under the null hypothesis of zero excess co-movement ($\sigma_N^2 = 0$) the t-ratio is asymptotically $N(0,1)$.

The results of the simulation experiments for a variety of sample sizes (T) and values of σ_N^2 (and the implied correlation between the two disturbances) are given in Table 3.1. Here, PR denotes the test of Pindyck and Rotemberg, and LLR denotes our test.

Table entries represent the empirical probabilities of rejecting the null hypothesis of no excess co-movement (power) at the nominal 5

Table 3.1   *Power comparisons of tests for excess co-movement*
                (1,000 replications)

σ_N^2	0.00	0.05	0.10	0.15	0.20	0.25	0.30	0.40	0.60	0.80
corr $(v_{1,t}, v_{2,t})$	0.00	0.05	0.09	0.13	0.17	0.20	0.23	0.29	0.38	0.44
T = 100										
LLR	0.05	0.08	0.15	0.27	0.39	0.51	0.63	0.80	0.97	1.00
PR	0.05	0.14	0.20	0.29	0.42	0.52	0.60	0.71	0.94	1.00
T = 200										
LLR	0.05	0.10	0.23	0.44	0.65	0.80	0.90	0.98	1.00	1.00
PR	0.05	0.15	0.26	0.44	0.61	0.75	0.83	0.96	1.00	1.00
T = 400										
LLR	0.05	0.15	0.45	0.73	0.90	1.00	1.00	1.00	1.00	1.00
PR	0.05	0.22	0.45	0.70	0.83	0.93	0.98	1.00	1.00	1.00

per cent critical value of a $N(0,1)$ distribution. Both tests appear to have the correct levels under the null hypothesis and the power of the tests increases rapidly with departures from the null hypothesis and with increasing sample size. Note that for the large sample sizes even relatively small degrees of correlation are detected with high probability. Broadly speaking, when both tests have less than 50 per cent power, PR's test is superior. On the other hand when the power of both tests is above 50 per cent then our test dominates. Both tests have very high power for high correlations. These features are illustrated in Figure 3.1, which plots the power curves of both tests reported in Table 3.1 for a sample of 200.

It should be noted that in the foregoing analysis we have abstracted from complications that would have arisen had we adopted the full sequential testing procedure of first testing for co-integration between prices and macroeconomic variables and co-integration between the two prices. We have also, in applying the PR test, avoided testing for the significance of the included macro-economic variables. In both cases, application of the full procedures would affect both the true significance level and the power of the tests for excess co-movement.

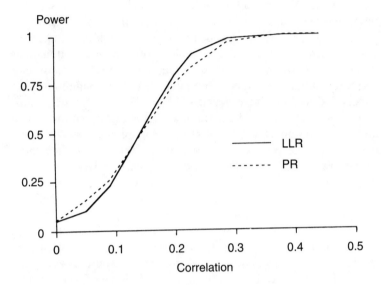

Figure 3.1: The Power of the Tests

3.5 CONCLUDING REMARKS

It is observed that commodity prices have a tendency to move together over time. This co-movement of commodity prices is attributed to the impact of macroeconomic influences that are common to all prices. Previous research has focused on the presence of excess co-movement in commodity prices, i.e. price correlation over and above that which can be explained by the effects of common macroeconomic variables. However, the empirical evidence is contradictory, possibly reflecting the different approaches that have been employed in testing the excess co-movement hypothesis, and it is to the methodology of testing that this paper contributes. Using stylized versions of previous approaches we find that the test adopted by Pindyck and Rotemberg (1990) performs well from a statistical standpoint when the model is correctly specified. It suffers, we argue, in comparison with our preferred approach in not permitting testing of the model specification, since if the model is under-specified with a common variable omitted then (spurious) excess co-movement follows automatically. In addition, we find the test adopted by Palaskas and Varangis (1991) inappropriate, since it is biased to rejection of the null hypothesis of no excess co-movement and thus is not a useful test for excess co-movement. Consequently, the validity of their empirical findings is cast into doubt. We also contend that definitional imprecision of co-movement and excess co-movement is a failing common to both papers. To address these deficiencies we offer specific definitions from which a simple unified framework for testing co-movement and excess co-movement follows. We propose a necessarily rigorous definition of price *co-movement* in that prices *co-move* if those prices are both co-integrated and their partial derivatives with respect to each I(1) variable have the same sign. Such co-movement refers to common I(1) ('long run') behaviour whereas excess co-movement refers to common I(0) ('short-run') behaviour. Phrasing terms in this way clarifies the distinction between co-movement and excess co-movement. The testing procedure we advocate is tractable and should minimize the occurence of spurious excess co-movement that may have influenced the findings of Pindyck and Rotemberg. Whether excess co-movement in commodity prices is a real phenomenon or merely an artefact of their approach has yet to be determined, and is the focus of ongoing empirical research.

APPENDIX

That the PV approach cannot provide a valid text for excess co-movement may be demonstrated by considering its asymptotic properties when applied to the following simple model. Let

$$P_{1,t} = \alpha X_{1,t} + \varepsilon_{1,t} \qquad (A3.1)$$

$$P_{2,t} = X_{1,t} + \varepsilon_{2,t} \qquad (A3.2)$$

$$X_{1,t} = X_{1,t-1} + \eta_t \qquad (A3.3)$$

for $t = 1, \ldots, T$ and where $\varepsilon_{1,t} \sim$ iid $(0,\sigma_1^2)$, $\varepsilon_{2,t} \sim$ iid $(0,\sigma_2^2)$ $\eta_t \sim$ iid $(0,\sigma_\eta^2)$. The error correction model for (A3.1) and (A3.2) has the form

$$\Delta P_{1,t} = \alpha \Delta P_{2,t} - (P_{1,t-1} - \alpha P_{2,t-1}) + (\varepsilon_{1,t} - \alpha \varepsilon_{2,t}) \qquad (A3.4)$$

PV would add $\Delta X_{1,t}$ as an additional regressor in this equation, which implies that (A3.4) must be rewritten as

$$\Delta P_{1,t} = \alpha \Delta P_{2,t} - (P_{1,t-1} - \alpha P_{2,t-1}) +$$
$$\beta \Delta X_{1,t} + (\varepsilon_{1,t} - \alpha \varepsilon_{2,t} - \beta \eta_t) \qquad (A3.5)$$

Since we can obtain a T-consistent estimate[4] of $(P_{1,t-1} - \alpha P_{2,t-1})$ from the co-integrating regression, for the purposes of this exposition we can assume that (asymptotically) it is known. Hence, defining

$$Y_t = \Delta P_{1,t} + (P_{1,t-1} - \alpha P_{2,t-1}) \qquad (A3.6)$$

allows us to write (A3.5) as

$$Y_t = \alpha^* \Delta P_{2,t} + \beta^* \Delta X_{1,t} + \varepsilon_t^*, \text{ where}$$
$$\varepsilon_t^* = \varepsilon_{1,t} - \alpha \varepsilon_{2,t} - \beta^* \eta_t \qquad (A3.7)$$

Now consider estimating (A3.7) by OLS, denoting the estimated coefficient on $\Delta P_{2,t}$ as $\hat{\alpha}^*$, and that on $\Delta X_{1,t}$ as $\hat{\beta}^*$. We shall concentrate on $\hat{\alpha}^*$, which according to PV will be driven to zero by the inclusion of $\Delta X_{1,t}$ as a regressor. We may write the OLS estimator of α^* as

$$\hat{\alpha}^* = \alpha^* + \frac{\sum_t \Delta X_{1,t}^2 \sum_t \Delta P_{2,t} \varepsilon_t^* - \sum_t \Delta P_{2,t} \Delta X_{1,t} \sum_t \Delta X_{1,t} \varepsilon_t^*}{\sum_t \Delta X_{1,t}^2 \sum_t \Delta P_{2,t}^2 - (\sum_t \Delta X_{1,t} \Delta P_{2,t})^2}$$

Now

$$\frac{1}{T} \sum_t \Delta P_{2,t}^2 = \frac{1}{T} \left(\sum_t \Delta X_{1,t} + \Delta \varepsilon_{2,t} \right)^2$$

$$= \frac{1}{T} \left(\sum_t \eta_t + \varepsilon_{2,t} - \varepsilon_{2,t-1} \right)^2$$

$$= \frac{1}{T} \sum_t \eta_t^2 + \frac{1}{T} \sum_t \varepsilon_{2,t}^2 + \frac{1}{T} \sum_t \varepsilon_{2,t-1}^2 + o_P(1)$$

$$\xrightarrow{P} \sigma_\eta^2 + 2\sigma_2^2$$

Similarly,

$$\frac{1}{T} \sum {}_t \Delta X_{1,t}^2 \xrightarrow[P]{} \sigma_\eta^2$$

$$\frac{1}{T} \sum {}_t \Delta X_{1,t} \Delta P_{2,t} \xrightarrow[P]{} \sigma_\eta^2$$

$$\frac{1}{T} \sum {}_t \Delta P_{2,t} \varepsilon_t^* \xrightarrow[P]{} -\alpha \sigma_2^2 - \beta \sigma_\eta^2$$

$$\frac{1}{T} \sum {}_t \Delta X_{1,t} \varepsilon_t^* \xrightarrow[P]{} -\beta \sigma_\eta^2$$

It follows that

$$\hat{\alpha}^* \xrightarrow[P]{} \alpha^* + \frac{\sigma_\eta^2(-\alpha\sigma_2^2 - \beta\sigma_\eta^2) - \sigma_\eta^2(-\beta\sigma_\eta^2)}{(\sigma_\eta^2 + 2\sigma_2^2)\,\sigma_\eta^2 - (\sigma_\eta^2)^2}$$

or

$$\hat{\alpha}^* \xrightarrow[P]{} \alpha^* - \frac{1}{2}\alpha$$

We may show in the same manner that

$$\hat{\beta}^* \xrightarrow[P]{} \beta^* + \frac{1}{2}\alpha - \beta$$

However, we know that $\alpha^* = \alpha$ and $\beta^* = \beta$, and therefore

$$\hat{\alpha}^* \xrightarrow[P]{} \alpha - \frac{1}{2}\alpha = \frac{1}{2}\alpha$$

$$\hat{\beta}^* \xrightarrow[P]{} \beta + \frac{1}{2}\alpha - \beta = \frac{1}{2}\alpha$$

In other words, inclusion of $\Delta X_{1,t}$ in the error correction model does not drive the estimated coefficient on $\Delta P_{2,t}$ to zero, since the probability limit of $\hat{\alpha}^*$ is non-zero. Their approach would therefore be unable to identify the presence of excess co-movement in this simple model. A parallel but more complicated analysis shows that in the more general case, where the ECM component is estimated rather than assumed to be known, a similar result holds.

NOTES

1. Despite their approach being biased into rejection of the null of no excess co-movement, Palaskas and Varangis rarely discover the presence of excess co-movement in practice. Since we are only interested in methodological issues in this paper and their approach is shown theoretically to be inappropriate, we do not attempt to account for this anomaly any further.
2. If the two prices cointegrate then a different sign on their partial derivatives with respect to one of the macroeconomic variables implies a different sign on their partial derivatives with respect to any other macroeconomic variable.
3. The notation '*nid*' means 'normally and independently distributed'.
4. That is, estimates of parameters converge to their true values at a rate inversely proportional to T rather than $\sqrt{T}$ (This property is known as 'super-consistency' – see Stock (1987)).

REFERENCES

Alogoskoufis, G., C. Martin and N. Pittis (1990): 'Pricing and product market structure in open economics', Discussion paper in Economics, 25/90, Birbeck College, University of London.

Engle, R.F. and C.W.J. Granger (1987): 'Co-integration and error correction: representation, estimation, and testing', *Econometrica*, **55**, 251–76.

Palaskas, T.B. and P.N. Varangis (1991): 'Is there excess co-movement of primary commodity prices?: a co-integration test', Working Paper Series no. 758, (International Economics Department, The World Bank).

Pindyck, R.S. and J.J. Rotemberg (1990): 'The excess co-movement of commodity prices', *Economic Journal*, **100**, 1173–89.

Stock, J. (1987): 'Asymptotic properties of least squares estimators of co-integrating vectors', *Econometrica*, **55**, 1035–56.

4. Stabilizing Earnings in Volatile Commodity Markets: Production Controls Versus Price Stabilization*

A.J. Hughes Hallett*

4.1 INTRODUCTION

This paper analyses how the statistical distribution of a producer's earnings in a primary commodity market would change with price stabilization or production controls. Commodity market stabilization agreements have been a major policy issue since the mid-1970s, both because commodity prices are so volatile and because exports of primary commodities are vitally important for generating foreign exchange, development funds and employment in the less developed countries (LDCs).

On the other hand, much of the trade and processing of commodities lies in the hands of the developed economies. The LDCs have therefore sought stabilization agreements in which, *inter alia*, prices would be higher on average, or more stable, and would redistribute resources from consumers in the 'North' to producers in the 'South'. A major difficulty with these proposals has been confusion over what the proper objectives of such a stabilization agreement should be. The producers and the international agencies tend to argue that the sheer volatility of prices is the main problem (UNCTAD, 1976). Alternative, but necessarily incompatible, objectives that have been put forward include stabilizing

* I am grateful to Chris Gilbert for comments and access to the Deaton-Laroque model software used in the Monte Carlo tests quoted in this paper, and to Yue Ma for his comments

producers' revenues, raising average prices, and improving the functioning of the market, or securing greater certainty of supply. This ambiguity over objectives is evident from the claim, made by the influential Brandt commission, that:[1] 'Commodity prices should be stabilised at a renumerative level to become less vulnerable to market fluctuations'. In a similar vein the main UNCTAD proposal (the Integrated Programme for Commodities; UNCTAD, 1976) did not make clear whether stabilized prices, stabilized incomes, or improved terms of trade were to be the objective of policy. It argued for '... stable conditions in commodity trade, including avoidance of excess price fluctuations, at levels which would ... be renumerative ... to producers and equitable to consumers'.

Recently there has been a revival of interest in explaining the volatility of commodity prices. Inevitably this has had the effect of raising the issue of the consequences, for producers' revenues, of stabilizing those prices. That concern can be found in recent work that has focused on the links between commodity market behaviour and macroeconomic performance (e.g. Moutos and Vines, 1989). Others (e.g. Gilbert, 1990; Gilbert and Palaskas, 1990; Trevedi, 1990) have concentrated on the interactions between commodity prices, inflation, exchange rates and other financial variables. However, the main developments have come from a re-evaluation of the theory of commodity price determination that pays particular attention to the price distributions which that theory generates (Deaton and Laroque, 1992). The theory of commodity prices may be well developed, but in the past there has been very little research that confronts that theory with evidence on the actual behaviour of prices. Deaton and Laroque argue that to the extent that theory does not explain actual price behaviour, then the theory must be modified so that it generates price distributions with the persistent autocorrelations, variability, asymmetries and kurtosis that we, in fact, observe. Those are the crucial features.

This paper complements the Deaton–Laroque approach by looking at the implications of their distributional analysis for stabilizing commodity revenues. Using the same kind of price and quantity distributions, both as theoretical constructs and in empirical form, we can identify the effects of two possible stabilization measures – price stabilization and production controls. Of the two, price stabilization appears to be more powerful. However, the main result is that any of these stabilization measures will generate conflicts in that greater earnings stability has to be 'bought' with lower average earnings. Thus the simple aims expressed by the Brandt Commission cannot be met (unless both instruments are used together in certain combinations). Moreover, production controls, unlike price stabilization, may also increase the probability of periods with low earnings or with large (rather than small) disturbances to earnings.

This paper, however, makes no attempt to establish the welfare case for stabilization. Since agricultural price supports and other market stabilization programmes exist in so many countries, our purpose is to demonstrate instead what outcomes of stabilization can be expected once the necessary welfare evaluations have been made and where producers merely wish to determine the best way of achieving that stabilization.

4.2 MATCHING THEORETICAL DISTRIBUTIONS WITH THE DATA: PRICES, OUTPUT AND STORAGE

The modelling strategy adopted in this paper is to suppose that market prices and the quantities traded follow underlying probability distributions that are invariant in the sense that the families of density functions, from which they are drawn, are determined by the structure of the market, rather than by external circumstances or by the particular decision rules adopted by market agents. The parameters of those distributions, however, are not invariant to exogenous events or changes in agents' decision rules. Deaton and Laroque (1992) show that such an approach allows a theoretical modelling strategy, based on the interactions of supply, demand and competitive storage, which generates results that match the stylized facts of high price variability; persistent autocorrelation in prices; plus skewness, kurtosis, and upwardly unbounded prices. It also allows for flexible distributions for quantities between fixed upper and lower bounds. All these results are obtained without having to resort to artificial or ad hoc assumptions such as attributing fluctuations to supply shocks, or to inelastic and/or non-linear demand functions, or to myopic demand or supply behaviour. Hence the *form* of the price distribution (and that is the crucial assumption in what follows) will be unaffected by the different numerical values that the supply and demand parameters, or external variables such as interest rates, may take.

As far as earnings stabilization is concerned, the important point is that a strong positive skew in the price distribution implies that prices tend to spend longer periods below average, interspersed with shorter periods of very high prices. That, married with the persistence of highly variable prices, will mean that there is a higher probability of large, rather than small, disturbances from the average price level. The stylized facts to be matched by the production model are a lot less clear, and vary from market to market in any case. So for quantities we take an entirely flexible distributional form, specifying no more than compact supports at the upper and lower bounds, and allow the data to determine the precise shape (skew, etc) of the supply distribution. Thus, subject to the existence of upper and lower bounds, almost any probability shape will do: our results will not be sensitive to the assumptions on the supply side either.

This pattern of price and supply behaviour at any particular moment, as Deaton and Laroque's model demonstrates formally, arises through the natural asymmetries of stockholding. The reason for this is that, given sufficient finance, it is relatively easy to build up stocks. Agents may not wish to accumulate stocks indefinitely, but the demand for stocks will nonetheless tend to hold prices up in periods of low demand. However, if stocks are low when demand is high, prices will exhibit sharp peaks as stocks become exhausted. Hence prices typically fall by considerably less in slumps than they rise in periods of excess demand. Empirical work has argued that mechanism plays an important role in shaping market behaviour (Wright and Williams, 1982; Hughes Hallett, 1986), and it is the same non-linearity that enables theoretical supply and demand models to explain the actual behaviour of prices and quantities in a natural way (Deaton and Laroque, 1992).

Similarly one might suppose that limited finance, and hence limits to the size of the stocks held, would imply that larger price shocks could be modified proportionately less than smaller shocks. That would lead to a degree of kurtosis, in addition to any asymmetries. Kurtosis may be more marked in the foreign exchange and financial markets, but we should expect it in commodity prices too.

In selecting particular probability specifications for examination, we have to be guided by the stylized or observed facts. We take prices to be described by a Gamma distribution. That reflects the facts pretty well. Prices are not restricted apart from being positive. This distribution also supplies a strong positive skew and a (somewhat weaker) positive kurtosis, which is consistent with the stockholding behaviour described above since it implies occasional sharp peaks and somewhat more persistent periods of low prices, plus a propensity to large shocks. More important, the Gamma distribution fits the data rather well (see Section 4.4 below). In fact, and this is perhaps decisive, the shape matches very closely that obtained from Deaton and Laroque's preferred theoretical model with isoelastic demand functions and competitive storage.[2] We cannot demonstrate an exact match because the complementary slackness discontinuities, in the supply from (or additions to) stocks, make it impossible to derive a closed form expression for the equilibrium price function, even when the underlying demand function is invertible and the supply function linear (as in the Deaton–Laroque model). That has been recognized since the work of Gustafson (1958), and it implies that we cannot derive an analytic expression for the density function of prices even in the simplest cases. However, Monte Carlo tests of the Deaton–Laroque model allow us to check numerically whether prices are theoretically distributed according to a Gamma distribution. For example, with a sample size of 200, a standard normal distribution for the log of production supplies, a real interest rate of 3 per cent, a demand elasticity of 0.33, and a lagged expected supply elasticity of 0.25, a conventional chi-squared goodness of fit test implied the resulting price distribution could be accepted as a Gamma distribution with probability value 88 per cent.[3] Having established that, we can fit a Gamma distribution directly to the price data. Furthermore, given the invariance property incorporated in Deaton and Laroque's model, this result cannot be sensitive to the particular parameter values used in the test.

For quantities, we have less to go on and have chosen a Beta distribution to match the stylized facts cited earlier. That distribution is non-negative and has the required compact upper and lower supports. Artificially truncating a normal distribution (the Deaton–Laroque procedure) is not necessary, therefore. In addition to that extra generality, this distribution also has the flexibility to assume a wide variety of different shapes with regard to supply variability, skew (of either sign this time) and kurtosis. These characteristics are determined by (direct estimates of) the absolute and relative sizes of its two main parameters.

4.3 REVENUE STABILITY AND THE EARNINGS DISTRIBUTION

The Distribution of Commodity Earnings

Let p = the current market price and q = quantity sold, so that earnings are given by $y = pq$. Next suppose p follows a Gamma distribution with parameters a and b, and that q independently follows a Beta distribution with parameters c and d (where $d = a - c$) together with a scale parameter m which represents the maximum possible level of production for a 'small' producer.[4] Then earnings, y, will be defined by a Gamma distribution with parameters c and $\lambda = b/m$:

Lemma 1:   Let $f(p) = p^{a-1}e^{-bp}/\Gamma(a,b)$ for $0 \leq p \leq \infty$ (4.1)

and $f(q) = (q/m)^{c-1}(1 - q/m)^{d-1}/[mB(c,d]$ with $0 \leq q \leq m$ (4.2)

be the density functions of two independent random variables p and q.

Then $y = pq$ has probability density

$f(y) = y^{c-1}e^{-\lambda y}/\Gamma(c,\lambda)$ where $\lambda = b/m$ and $0 \leq y \leq \infty$.

Proof: If $p \sim \Gamma(a,b)$, then $u = b_p$ has the standardized Gamma density function $\Gamma(a,1)$ defined by $f(u) = [b^a\Gamma(a,b)]^{-1}u^{a-1}e^{-u}$. Similarly if $q \sim B(c,d,m)$ then $v = y/m$ has the standardized Beta density function, defined on the interval [0,1] by $f(v) = [B(c,d)]^{-1}v^{c-1}(1 - v)^{d-1}$. If in addition $d = a - c > 0$, and p and q are independent random variables, then Aitchinson (1963) shows that $w = uv$ is distributed as a $\Gamma(c,1)$ variable: i.e. $f(w) = [\Gamma(c,1)]^{-1}w^{c-1}e^{-w}$ with $0 \leq w \leq \infty$. But $w = (b/m) y = \lambda y$. Hence y is distributed as

$$f(y) = (\lambda^c/\Gamma(c,1))y^{c-1}e^{-\lambda z} \quad 0 \geq y \geq \infty \quad (4.3)$$

which proves the result.

Armed with this result one can look at the mean and variance of the earnings distribution, together with other characteristics such as the coefficient of variation, skew and kurtosis, to see how they are related to the corresponding moments of the underlying price and quantity distributions.

For the most part, commodity producers will be interested in the mean, $\bar{y}$, and standard deviation of earnings, σ_y, as indicators of the expected level and volatility of their revenues. However, they will also be interested in some further indicators. For example, if there is any conflict in the sense that stabilizing earnings would reduce their average level of the same time, then producers will need to know if the coefficient of earnings variation, $\sigma_y / \bar{y}$, is going to rise or fall. That determines whether stabilization is worthwhile or not: would σ_y fall faster than $\bar{y}$, or vice versa? Similarly they will need to know whether stabilization would increase the degree of skew since, if it does, the probability of getting lower than average earnings will have increased (and the probability of higher than average earnings decreased). Longer or more frequent periods with low earnings may imply extra difficulties for producers even if the uncertainty surrounding their future revenues can be reduced at the same time. Indeed it can be plausibly argued that the aim of policy, particularly for the indebted developing economies, should be to prevent price troughs and periods of low earnings rather than to stabilize or raise average revenues as such (Gilbert, 1977; Hughes Hallet, 1984). Finally, it will be important to know whether the degree of kurtosis has increased since, if it has, the probability of large deviations of earnings from their average level will have increased, compared with the probability of getting only small disturbances.

Stabilization by Price Interventions and Production Controls

Table 4.1 summarizes the first two moments, together with the coefficients of variation, skew and kurtosis, of the price, quantity and earnings distributions under lemma 1. It is obvious that the objectives of earnings stability and their level, as well as the coefficients of variation, skew or kurtosis, are not affected by the price distribution parameter a or the production distribution parameter d. That leaves two strategies. The first possibility is a price stabilization strategy; increasing the value of b, by setting firm or 'soft' support prices, or by establishing a buffer stock intervention

Table 4.1 The effect of different earnings stabilization strategies

(a) Prices: distributed as $\Gamma(a,b)$

moments		Effect of: reducing a	increasing b	with multiplier of
mean $\bar{p}$	$= a/b$	falls	falls	$-a/b^2$
variance σ_p^2	$= a/b^2$	falls	falls	$-2a/b^3$
mode	$= (a-1)/b$	falls	falls	$-(a-1)/b^2$
coefficient of variation $= \sigma_p/\bar{p}$	$= 1/\sqrt{a}$	rises	no change	0
of skew $= \mu_3/\sigma_p^3$	$= 2/\sqrt{a}$	rises	no change	0
of kurtosis $= \mu_4/\sigma_p^4 - 3$	$= 6/a$	rises	no change	0

Table 4.1 The effect of different earnings stabilization strategies continued

(b) Quantities: distributed as B(c,d,m) where d = a–c

moments		Effect of: reducing a	increasing b	with multiplier of
mean $\bar{q}$	$= mc/a$	falls	falls	m/a
variance σ_q^2	$\dfrac{m^2 c\,(a-c)}{(a+1)a^2}$	falls	falls if $a \geq 2c$	$m^2(a-2c)/((a+1)a^2)$
mode	$= m\,(c-1)/(a-2)$	falls	falls if $a \geq 2$	$m/(a-2)$
coefficient of variation	$\sigma_q/\bar{q} = \sqrt{(a-c)/((a+1)c)}$	no change	rises	$\tfrac{1}{2}a[c^3(a+1)(a-c)]^{-1/2}$
of skew	$\mu_3/\sigma q^3 = \dfrac{2(a-2c)}{a+2}\sqrt{\dfrac{a+1}{(a-c)c}}$	no change	rises	$\dfrac{-a^2}{(a+2)}\sqrt{\dfrac{a+1}{(a-c)^3\,c^3}}$

Note: d ≥ 0 implies a ≥ c in every case.

Table 4.1 The effect of different earnings stabilization strategies continued

(c) Earnings: distributed as $\Gamma(c,\lambda)$ where $\lambda = b/m$

moments	Price stabilization		Production controls			
	increase b	with multiplier of	reduce m	with multiplier	reduce c	with multiplier
mean $\bar{y}$ = cm/b	falls	$-cm/b^2$	falls	c/b	falls	m/b
variance $\sigma_y^2 = cm^2/b^2$	falls	$-2cm^2/b^3$	falls	2cm/b	falls	$2cm/b^2$
mode = (c − 1)m/b	falls	$-(c-1)m/b$	falls	$(c-1)/b^2$	falls	m/b
coefficient of variation $\sigma_y/\bar{y} = 1/\sqrt{c}$	no change	0	no change	0	rises	$\tfrac{1}{2}\sqrt{c^3}$
of skew $= \mu_3/\sigma^3 y = 2/\sqrt{c}$	no change	0	no change	0	rises	$-1/\sqrt{c^3}$
kurtosis $= \mu_4/\delta^4 y = 6/c$	no change	0	no change	0	rises	$-6/c^2$

scheme, will stabilize prices and stabilize earnings in the process. But unfortunately price stabilization will also have the effect of reducing the mean price and average earnings at the same time. There is an inevitable conflict between the two primary targets, although the coefficient of earnings variation is not affected because the index of stability improves at the same rate as the average earnings level falls. The same holds for the coefficient of price variation. So there is a one-to-one trade-off between targets under this strategy; earnings can be stabilized through price stabilization schemes, but only with an equivalent loss in average earnings. On the other hand there is no increase in the earnings skew or kurtosis. So the chances of getting periods of lower than average earnings are not increased; nor are the probabilities of getting large rather than small shocks to the earnings stream.

The second stabilization strategy is to use production controls. There are two possibilities here – to set production (or export) ceilings, or to control the quantities supplied as a proportion of full capacity production. Production ceilings are set simply by m, while supply quotas are set by c since that controls the expected production level, $\bar{q}$, as a proportion of full capacity (recall d = a–c).[5] Thus, to stabilize earnings, we have to restrict supplies by reducing either m or c. That will have the effect not only of reducing earnings variability, but also of reducing average earnings at the same time – just as in the price stabilization case. So production controls do not allow us to escape this conflict. Indeed the production ceiling approach produces very similar results to the price stabilization strategy; a one-to-one trade-off between stability improvements and reductions in average earnings, such that the coefficient of earnings variation, as well as the coefficients of earnings skew and kurtosis, are unchanged. Supply quotas, on the other hand, lead to an unfavourable trade-off in that our index of earnings stability improves more slowly than average earnings fall, so there is a rise in the coefficient of earnings variation; and the coefficients of skew and kurtosis also rise indicating that this strategy would increase the chances of periods with low earnings, or with large disturbances to revenues. In that sense quotas represent an inferior strategy to both production ceilings and price stabilization.[6]

There is of course a third strategy of attempting to stabilize revenues by hedging output on the futures markets. The difficulty with that approach, as with the formal welfare arguments which underlie it, is that it presumes a sufficiently large set of contingency markets exist for each commodity (Gilbert, 1985). In practice few commodities possess a comprehensive set of such markets, and in many cases no contingency markets exist at all. In any case it is doubtful if producers in the smaller or indebted LDCs could secure the credit necessary to operate on such markets successfully. For these reasons we do not consider hedging strategies here.[7] Indeed the implication of the modelling approach outlined in Section 4.2 is that we should focus on the more limited question of what can be done with existing market structures.

Price Stabilization Versus Production Restrictions

Table 4.1 also shows the relative effectiveness of each of the possible earnings stabilization strategies in the form of multipliers defined as the partial derivative of the relevant moment or indicator with respect to the parameter being manipulated. Thus $\partial \bar{y}/\partial b = -cm/b^2$, $\partial \sigma_y^2/\partial m = 2cm/b^2$, $\partial skew(y)/\partial c = -c^{-3/2}$ and so on. If the multipliers are larger under one strategy than another then we can say that the strategy is more powerful as a stabilizing instrument – although that does not imply that it would also be as cheap or easy to obtain the necessary changes in parameter values under the given strategy. Where we are not concerned with the costs of operating each instrument, or where we can assume them to be roughly equal, we would clearly prefer the more powerful strategy. Otherwise we would have to trade-off effectiveness against intervention costs in the usual way.[8]

Inspection of Table 4.1 shows that, of the two production control schemes, setting production ceilings is more effective than introducing supply quotas for the two primary targets so long as $c > m$; a condition which is *unlikely* to hold in practice unless the production distribution is very tightly packed against the full capacity value, and which is obviously *not* satisfied in any of the empirical distributions reported in Table 4.4. Moreover such a large value for c would imply that earnings stabilization would have to be accompanied by an increased uncertainty about supplies. That probably adds to the difficulty of using any form of production control since the more effective strategy has the more unfavourable mean-variance earnings trade-off, and worse skew and kurtosis implications. However, this conflict with the earlier results does not really matter since price stabilization is more effective than either form of production control so long as $c/b > 1$ and $m/b > 1$ respectively. Those inequalities are almost certain to hold since commodity prices are extremely volatile, which means that b has to be less than unity to produce a large variance with a moderate average price (see Table 4.1, part (a)) – and if it doesn't, there is no problem to be solved. In fact both inequalities are satisfied by a wide margin in the empirical distributions which follow. Hence price stabilization is the most effective strategy, and it has no disadvantages in terms of the mean-variance trade-off or the skew and kurtosis implications.

Mean-Variance Strategies: Can Earnings Be Stabilized at a Higher Level?

The final question then is, can we also raise earnings while stabilizing them? In view of Tinbergen's theory of economic policy, stabilizing earnings at the same time as raising their average level would require the use of both price stabilization and a production control instrument. Suppose we take supply quotas. Then, by Table 4.1, $d\bar{y} > 0$ but $d\sigma_y^2 < 0$ can be achieved by picking db and dc to solve

$$\begin{bmatrix} -cm/b^2 & m/b \\ -2cm^2/b^3 & m^2/b^2 \end{bmatrix} \begin{bmatrix} db \\ dc \end{bmatrix} = \begin{bmatrix} > 0 \\ < 0 \end{bmatrix} \tag{4.4}$$

This can always be arranged since the determinant, $cm^3/b^4 \neq 0$, guarantees the existence of a solution. In fact, to solve Equation 4.4, db and dc must be chosen to satisfy

$$c/b \cdot db < dc < 2c/b \, db, \text{ or } 1 < \frac{dc}{db} \cdot \frac{b}{c} < 2. \tag{4.5}$$

Thus to resolve the conflict between the level of earnings and their stability, we have to operate both stabilization instruments, but one of them in the opposite way to which it would be used if it were taken in isolation; in this case, to increase b as well as c. That would involve a programme of price stabilization plus carefully controlled *increases* in planned (or average) supplies.[9] An important advantage of this combined approach, however, is that the degree of earnings skew and kurtosis will be reduced for the first time – so that the secondary aims of reducing the chances of low earnings, or large shocks in earnings, will also be achieved.

In practice policy-makers have favoured price stabilization measures, reserving production controls for difficult circumstances. Nevertheless production controls have been invoked in quite a number of cases. Price stabilization agreements have operated in the cocoa and natural rubber markets, and were proposed for UNCTAD's Integrated Commodity Programme. Production (export) restrictions have been used in the coffee, sugar and oil markets. Only the tin agreement used both instruments systematically and was quite successful in simultaneously raising and stabilizing prices until its collapse in 1985. Similarly the largest stabilization schemes, those for agricultural produce, have typically used a combination of price supports and production quotas (at least in Europe's Common Agricultural Policy and in the US's farm policy). That too has raised and stabilized prices at the same time, at some cost to the taxpayer. Note that explicit price supports are already automatically covered by our analysis since truncating the price distribution merely scales the original distribution up over its reduced range (Johnson and Kotz, 1970). That will certainly have the effect of increasing average prices *and* reducing their variance in the case of a minimum price support. However, it also implies that all our analysis goes through unchanged from Lemma 1, where p is now interpreted as deviations from the price support, since the form of Equation 4.1 is unchanged.

4.4   THE EMPIRICAL EVIDENCE

Data

We have examined price and earnings distribution for three commodities that are widely traded internationally and that are predominantly produced in developing countries. Of the 29 most important commodities reported in the World Bank's *Commodity Trade and Price Trends*, which also covers UNCTAD's 15 'core commodities', we selected copper, coffee and rubber as an illustration of the typical price and earnings distributions that primary commodity producers face.[10] Two of these commodities have been subject to price stabilization agreements and all three are predominantly produced in developing economies. In fact our selection of the three commodity markets was governed by three factors: high price/earnings volatility, a high dependence of LDC producers on earnings in those markets, and as something of a representative 'sample' of commodities (one metal and two perennial crops).

Table 4.2 sets out those characteristics for the major producers in these three markets. Price variability is measured here by the coefficient of variation of the US dollar price per unit, deflated by the UN's index of export unit values for manufactured goods. We used monthly data covering the period January 1973 to December 1987, compiled from the following sources:

Prices: UN's *Monthly Commodity Price Bulletins* and the IMF's *International Financial Statistics*.

Quantities: For coffee and rubber – FAO's *Monthly Bulletins on Agricultural Commodities'*. For copper – *Metal Statistics* (Metallgesellschaft A.G., Frankfurt-am-Main). The quantity data was available only as quarterly data. By considering the monthly export volumes of countries, which among them hold more than 60–70 per cent of the export markets of the respective commodities, the quarterly data was converted into monthly data.

The maximum coefficient of price variation across all 29 of the major commodities was 0.45; and for our three markets the coefficients were 0.44 per cent, 0.34 per cent and 0.38 per cent respectively, compared to figures of 0.06 to 0.10 for industrial goods. So the three markets that we have chosen satisfy the volatile prices criterion very well. Similarly, trade in those commodities is dominated by LDC producers, and the producers singled out here are heavily dependent on commodities for their export earnings. Finally the use of Gamma and Beta distributions to describe the underlying price and quantity distributions in this exercise was justified earlier. The empirical evidence provides further support for that proposition. Table 4.3 shows that every producer faces significant departures from normality – which invariably has been the alternative assumption – in either prices or quantities (and usually both) at the 1 per cent significance level. In fact if we look at the third and fourth moments separately, we find that all three prices are distributed with a significant positive skew (at the 1 per

Table 4.2 Price variability, trade participants and market concentration

Producer	Coefficient of price variation[a]	% Trade originating in LDCs (1981–87)	% Exports supplied by primary commodities[b]	Price/quantity correlation coefficient[c]
Copper: Zaire	} 0.44	} 63	94	0.04
Chile			92	-0.06
Coffee: Ivory Coast	} 0.34	} 91	90	0.11
Columbia			79	-0.11
Brazil			55	-0.16*
Rubber: Malaysia	} 0.38	} 99	61	0.11
Indonesia			72	0.26**
Thailand			47	-0.14
Sri Lanka			60	0.07

Notes:
(a) For comparisons, electrical machinery and equipment and clothing had coefficients of price variation of 0.06 and 0.08 respectively.
(b) * = approximately significant at the 5% level. ** = significant at the 1% level.
(c) In 1987.

Source: World Development Report 1989.

Table 4.3   Jarque-Bera tests of non-normality

Market				
Copper:	*prices* 92.08**	*quantity,*	Zaire	8.04*
			Chile	0.53
Coffee:	*prices* 22.97**	*quantity,*	Ivory Coast	7.94*
			Columbia	1.01
			Brazil	14.19**
Rubber:	*prices* 21.77**	*quantity,*	Malaysia	5.41
			Indonesia	109.33**
			Thailand	103.37**
			Sri Lanka	170.02**

Note:
Critical values of $\chi^2(2)$ at 5% is 5.99; at 1% is 9.21.
* = significant at 5%.
** = significant at 1% level.

cent level) but no obvious kurtosis; while the quantities tend to show significant positive skews *and* kurtosis. (These results appear in Tables A4.1 and A4.2 of the appendix.) It is appropriate therefore to fit a Gamma distribution to prices, and a Beta distribution with c > d to the quantities traded.

The remaining issue is the independence of those two distributions. A difficulty arises here because Table 4.3 shows that prices and quantities are not distributed normally so that a statistically negligible correlation between prices is only a necessary, but not a sufficient condition for establishing independence. In fact all but two of the producers show statistically insignificant correlations (Table 4.2). The remaining two cases show low correlations (marginally insignificant in the case of Brazilian coffee, but clearly significant for Indonesian rubber). The corresponding indices constructed from the higher order joint moments (to 4th order) were similarly small, but we are unable to test their statistical insignificance formally because the distributions of those indices are not known. Thus a potential weakness of this empirical evidence is that we have been unable to establish definitively that all price and quantity distributions are independent. Nevertheless our results are unlikely to be affected much, even if independence were rejected, since the ability of individual producers to influence prices systematically is evidently very small.

Estimation

We fit the parameters of the prices, quantities and earnings distributions (via lemma 1), for the nine producers in our three markets, by a generalized method of moments (GMM) technique. This technique involves fitting parameters for our probability model which, when simulated by random drawings run through that model, reproduce the empirically observed moments as closely as possible. That provides statistically consistent parameter estimates (Duffie and Singleton, 1989; Smith and Spencer, 1990; Deaton and Laroque, 1992). Following Smith and Spencer (1990), and Gregory and Smith (1990), we take

$$\min_{\theta} L = \sum_{r=1}^{q} [\mu_r(\theta)^{1/r} - m_r^{1/r}]^2 \qquad (4.6)$$

as the fitting criterion, where m_r is the observed rth central moment and $\mu_r(\theta)$ is the fitted rth central moment implied by parameter values, θ, and where there are q moments to be fitted. This is a quadratic loss function in the first q moments and differs from the Smith–Spencer approach only in being unweighted and because we set $q = 4$ instead of 3.[11] Equation 4.6 is however, a considerable simplification, from a computational point of view, on the Deaton–Laroque approach, which uses a conventional quadratic criterion weighted by an idempotent function of suitable instruments and then rewritten directly in terms of the parameters to be estimated. Monte Carlo tests of a variety of GMM estimators (including those mentioned here, and a maximum likelihood approach) revealed Equation 4.6 to be the most reliable (Hughes Hallett and Ma, 1993).

For the purposes of illustration we have retained the simplicity of the Smith–Spencer approach, which in our case has the further advantage that we do not have to specify the underlying supply, demand and stockholding functions explicitly and hence allows us to avoid the specification and fitting errors associated with those functions. To test the results, we can simulate the implications of the fitted parameters directly in the density functions. That is also the Gregory and Smith (1990) procedure, although it must be recognized as a somewhat informal technique for testing the adequacy of the model compared to the formal J-tests proposed by Hansen (1982) and the conventional overidentification tests used by Deaton and Laroque.

Stabilization Strategies

The results of our estimation procedure applied to the prices and earnings distributions are set out in Table 4.4, where the quantity distribution parameters follow by imposing the restrictions of lemma 1. The fitted distributions reproduce the observed data very well. The fitted and observed moments match one another fairly closely, as can be checked via the appendix, which gives low values of L in Equation 4.6. There are a couple of exceptions to that, such as Columbian coffee and Sri Lankan rubber where a particular moment fails to fit closely. Otherwise the fits are remarkably close, and the estimate parameters entirely plausible. The order parameters (a,c) are well above unity for prices and earnings, while the scale parameters (b,λ) are very small as expected. For prices this gives the hypothesized shape of a highly (positively) skewed distribution, with a clear mode and no great kurtosis in each one. The quantity distributions also have clear modes and are asymptotic to the axis at $q = 0$ and $q = m$ (since c > 2 and d > 2 by a reasonable margin, and since a > c). That implies a good deal of kurtosis. The quantity distributions display a variety of shapes with positive skews for Zairi copper, Ivory Coast and Brazilian coffee, and Thai and Sri Lankan rubber. Symmetry holds roughly for Chilean copper and Indonesian rubber; while negative skews are shown by Columbian coffee and Malaysian rubber. The positive skews suggest those producers were working well below capacity for much of the 1973–87 period – which is not surprising since these are the higher cost producers and commodity prices were very depressed during that period (the boom of 1973/4 excepted). Only the most efficient producers, or those with the newer and better equipped production facilities, would show a higher degree of capacity uilisation on average.

Given the empirical results in Table 4.4, one can compute the relative effectiveness of price stabilization versus production controls for stabilizing earnings. The multipliers needed for that

Table 4.4 *The results of fitting the prices and earnings distributions*

		Prices		Quantities			Earnings	
		a	b	c	d	m	c	$\lambda = b/m$
Copper:	Zaire	14.31	0.00893	3.970	10.340	53.15	3.970	0.000168
	Chile	"	"	7.014	7.296	115.97	7.014	0.000077
Coffee:	Ivory Coast	7.026	0.002465	2.055	4.971	70.43	2.055	0.000035
	Columbia	"	"	4.555	2.471	69.63	4.555	0.0000354
	Brazil	"	"	2.613	4.413	171.18	2.613	0.0000144
Rubber:	Malaysia	15.39	0.0167	9.515	5.875	210.06	9.515	0.0000795
	Indonesia	"	"	6.772	8.618	170.41	6.772	0.000098
	Thailand	"	"	3.885	11.505	172.16	3.885	0.000097
	Sri Lanka	"	"	2.415	12.975	660.08	2.415	0.0000253

comparison (taken from Table 4.1) are evaluated in Table 4.5. The first observation has to be that these policies are, in principle, very powerful.[12] The multipliers are large in comparison with the underlying moments, so that relatively small adjustments to the parameters in question would secure adjustment to the earnings distribution. That does not imply it is easy to engineer changes in b, c or m; only that the pay offs from doing so, in terms of mean or variance reductions, would be large. Secondly, our earlier analysis of Table 4.1 is confirmed. It is more effective to stabilize earnings via price stabilization than via production controls of either type. Also, as we noted in Table 4.1, reducing earnings variability implies a lower mean. But the $\partial \bar{y} / \partial V(y)$ trade-off shows that the damage done [in lower average earnings per unit reduction in earnings variability] is smaller under the price stabilization strategy than with output quotas in all but two cases (Zairi copper, Brazilian coffee). So that trade-off also favours price stabilization.

4.5   SUMMARY AND CONCLUSIONS

Using a simple model of the distribution of earnings in a commodity market, where both production and prices are subject to uncertainty, we found:

(a)   There will generally be a conflict between the two most frequently cited objectives of commodity and agricultural market stabilization agreements, namely that to stabilize producers' revenues will lead to lower revenues on average and vice versa.

(b)   In the present circumstances of underdeveloped contingency markets, two stabilization strategies are available – price stabilization or production controls. The latter may be implemented in the form of production ceilings or production quotas, with some differences in the outcomes. The former might involve minimum support prices or buffer stock interventions, but the differences would be immaterial in the context of this paper.

(c)   Both strategies will be needed if the conflict between stabilized and higher average earnings is to be resolved. That can always be done if the interventions are designed to satisfy the restric-

Table 4.5 *The multiplier effects on earnings from a unit change in the underlying parameter*

(a) Price stabilization (increase b)

on:	mean	variance	CV	skew	kurtosis
Copper:					
Zaire	-2.65×10^6	-3.15×10^{10}	–	–	–
Chile	-1.01×10^7	-2.65×10^{11}	–	–	–
Coffee:					
Ivory Coast	-2.38×10^7	-6.8×10^{11}	–	–	–
Columbia	-5.22×10^7	-2.95×10^{12}	–	–	–
Brazil	-7.36×10^7	-1.02×10^{13}	–	–	–
Rubber:					
Malaysia	-7.17×10^6	-1.80×10^{11}	–	–	–
Indonesia	-4.14×10^6	-8.44×10^{10}	–	–	–
Thailand	-2.40×10^6	-4.94×10^{10}	–	–	–
Sri Lanka	-5.72×10^6	-4.51×10^{11}	–	–	–

(b) Output quotas (reduce c)

	mean	variance	CV	skew	kurtosis
Copper:					
Zaire	$.595\times10^3$	-3.54×10^7	0.063	0.126	0.381
Chile	-1.30×10^4	-1.69×10^8	0.027	0.054	0.122
Coffee:					
Ivory Coast	-2.86×10^4	-8.18×10^8	0.017	0.339	1.420
Columbia	-2.82×10^4	-7.95×10^8	0.051	0.103	0.289
Brazil	-6.94×10^4	-4.82×10^9	0.118	0.237	0.879
Rubber:					
Malaysia	-1.26×10^4	-1.59×10^8	0.017	0.034	0.066
Indonesia	-1.02×10^4	-1.04×10^8	0.028	0.057	0.131
Thailand	-1.03×10^4	-1.06×10^8	0.065	0.131	0.397
Sri Lanka	-3.95×10^4	-1.56×10^9	0.035	0.071	1.029

Table 4.5 *The multiplier effects on earnings from a unit change in the underlying parameter (continued)*

(c) Production ceilings (reduce m)					
	mean	variance	CV	skew	kurtosis
Copper:					
Zaire	-4.45×10^2	-5.29×10^6	–	–	–
Chile	-7.85×10^2	-2.04×10^7	–	–	–
Coffee:					
Ivory Coast	-8.34×10^2	-4.76×10^7	–	–	–
Columbia	-1.85×10^3	-1.04×10^8	–	–	–
Brazil	-1.06×10^3	-1.47×10^8	–	–	–
Rubber:					
Malaysia	-5.98×10^2	-1.43×10^7	–	–	–
Indonesia	-4.06×10^2	-8.28×10^6	–	–	–
Thailand	-2.33×10^2	-4.77×10^6	–	–	–
Sri Lanka	-1.45×10^2	-1.14×10^7	–	–	–

tion in Equation 4.5. In that way, and only in that way, will the chances of getting periods of low earnings (or large shocks to earnings) also be reduced.

(d)   Of these two strategies, price stabilization is more effective (but not necessarily 'cheaper') than production controls from the point of view of stabilizing earnings without any adverse effects on the coefficients of earnings variation, or of increasing the chances of periods with low earnings and/or large disturbances to earnings.

(e)   This analysis has been designed to show the *marginal* impacts of introducing price stabilization or production controls, not the optimal amounts of each. That allows us to pick between strategies, but not to design particular intervention rules (in the sense of selecting an optimal buffer stock, price supports, or production ceilings, etc.) which might compromise our distributional *invariance* assumption. On the other hand, in terms of the Lucas critique, it doesn't matter if the intervention strategies do change the parameters of market behaviour so long as the 'deep' parameters – in this case the functional forms (but not parameter values) chosen for the underlying probability distributions – don't change. Given the very considerable flexibility in the probability distributions used here, such changes in the deep parameters are effectively ruled out unless the intervention rules are chosen in a way that gives market power to producers (individually or collectively). That would compromise the distributional *independence* assumption. To avoid that, these rules need to be designed by an independent market authority, rather than endogenously by some kind of producers' cooperative.

APPENDIX: TESTS OF NON-NORMALITY BY COMMODITY MARKET

Table A4.1

Skewness: $\delta_1 = 1/n\Sigma(y_i-\bar{y})^3/[1/n\Sigma(y_i-\bar{y})^2]^{3/2} = \mu_3/\sigma^3$
Kurtosis: $\delta_2 = [1/n\Sigma(y_i-\bar{y})^4/[1/n\Sigma(y_i-\bar{y}^2]^2]-3 = [\mu_4/\sigma^4]^3$

Market	Spot prices		Producer	Quantity traded	
	δ_1	δ_2		δ_1	δ_2
Coffee	0.613*	1.249	Ivory Coast	0.344**	–0.765
			Columbia	0.110	0.294
			Brazil	0.275	1.261
Rubber	0.724*	0.899	Malaysia	0.292	0.617
			Indonesia	1.149*	3.049*
			Sri Lanka	1.615*	3.498*
			Thailand	1.197*	2.999*
Copper	1.419*	2.055	Zaire	0.513*	0.139
			Chile	0.052	0.242

Note:
* Denotes significance at the 1% level, ** at the 5% level.

Table A4.2

	Copper Mean	Copper Variance	3rd moment	4th moment
Price: (US\$/MT) Quantity: (1,000MT)	1600.1	1.409×10^5	7.514×10^7	1.005×10^{11}
Zaire	14.69	44.56	152.99	6520.6
Chile	57.74	206.97	152.40	1.150×10^5
	Zaire	Chile		
μ_{21}	9.595	-5.96×10^5		
μ_{12}	-932.45	1.039×10^4		
μ_{22}	5.132×10^6	4.0435×10^7		
ρ	0.0407	-0.0624		

	Coffee Mean	Coffee Variance	3rd moment	4th moment
Price: (US\$/MT) Quantity: (1,000MT)	2852.3	1.158×10^6	7.639×10^8	5.698×10^{12}
Ivory Coast	20.54	104.23	366.09	2.428×10^4
Columbia	44.51	223.27	366.00	1.642×10^5
Brazil	65.42	740.82	5551.9	2.339×10^6
	Ivory Coast	Columbia	Brazil	
μ_{21}	2.336×10^6	-7.414×10^6	-3.482×10^4	
μ_{12}	6481.6	3.833×10^5	2.632×10^5	
μ_{22}	1.152×10^8	2.818×10^8	8.362×10^8	
ρ	0.113	-0.1094	-0.1589	

where $\mu_{ij} = E(p-\bar{p})^i(q-\bar{q})^j$
and $\rho = \mu_{11}/(\mu_{10}\mu_{01})^{1/2}$.

Table A4.2 (continued)

	Mean	Rubber Variance	3rd moment	4th moment
Price: (US$/MT)	919.6	50002.3	8.106×10^6	9.748×10^9
Quantity: (1,000MT)				
Malaysia	129.72	307.88	1577.53	3.429×10^5
Indonesia	73.26	156.90	2257.18	1.489×10^5
Sri Lanka	10.89	24.65	197.67	3948.3
Thailand	43.18	326.92	7072.87	6.412×10^5
	Malaysia	Indonesia	Sri Lanka	Thailand
μ_{21}	27310.7	27094.1	11117.37	-2.561×10^{11}
μ_{12}	5255.08	19241.8	96.62	-4652.14
μ_{22}	2.654×10^7	1.341×10^7	1.859×10^6	1.259×10^7
ρ	0.110	0.256	-0.139	0.067

NOTES

1. Brandt and co-authors (1980).
2. Table 2 and Figure 4 in Deaton and Laroque (1992).
3. The test used was the χ^2 test of Kendall and Stewart (vol. II, 1973, p. 438) and gave a value of $\chi^2 (7) = 3.06$ when a Gamma distribution was fitted to the simulated prices using the estimation technique defined by Equation 4.6. The critical value, at 5 per cent significance, for this test is 14.1. The corresponding likelihood ratio test of the fit (Kendall and Stewart, vol. II, 1973, p. 437) gave $\chi^2 (9) = 5.07$, against a 5 per cent critical value of 16.9. On either test the null hypothesis, Gamma distributed prices, can therefore be accepted with overwhelming confidence. This estimation procedure was then compared to the Smith and Spencer (1991) technique; the Deaton–Laroque version of Hansen's (1982) GMM technique; a two-parameter method of moments; and a full-blooded maximum likelihood technique. Every single one of these techniques produced Gamma estimates acceptable at the 10 per cent, 5 per cent and 1 per cent significance levels. The Equation 4.6 estimates produced the closest fit, followed by Deaton–Laroque and then Smith–Spencer, on the χ^2 criterion; and also the closest fit, followed by Smith–Spencer and then Deaton–Laroque, on the likelihood ratio criterion. The fact that the maximum likelihood estimator performed relatively badly is due to poor small sample properties and its sensitivity to outliers. Deaton and Laroque point out that the non-linearities in the model mean that *very* large samples are sometimes needed to obtain accurate estimates of the underlying invariant distribution. A sample size of 200 may look quite normal for econometric work, but it is not large if an estimator that is not robust in small samples is used. Hence the need to test this result with alternative estimators.

4. It is important to note that 'small' in this context means producers who are differentiated by supply conditions, geography, or by type or quality of product, as well as by negligible market power.

5. In either case, actual production/supply remains a random variable within the confines imposed by these parameters. Of course if production is not subject to random disturbances, due to the weather or strikes, etc. then there will be no distinction between these two production control strategies.

6. Reducing m also causes average supply to fall, one-to-one, with reductions in the index of supply instability, so that there is no change in the coefficients of supply variation and skew. The markets would probably be happier with this greater certainty of supply, than with reducing c, which reduces average supplies but may increase supply instability and certainty increases the coefficient of supply variation *and* skew and therefore raises the probability of unplanned shortages.

7. See Hughes Hallett and Ramanujam (1990) for a treatment of this aspect in a distribution free (i.e. non-normal) framework.

8. The effect of intervention costs on the optimal hedging or price stabilization strategies is examined in Hughes Hallett and Ramanujam (1990). They find that intervention costs are likely to influence the choice of strategy, and the degree of stabilization undertaken, for high unit value commodities. However, it is not clear if that result carries over to supply restrictions.

9. We can derive a parallel result for the production ceilings case, since the corresponding expression for Equation 4.4 has determinant $2 (1/b-1)m^2/b \neq 0$ if $b \neq 1$. We get $m/b^2db < 2m/b^2db$ to replace Equation 4.5, and hence the same implication that production controls have to be used in the opposite way than if they were to be operated in isolation.

10. The 'core commodities' were those thought by UNCTAD to be of prime significance in any stabilization programme. They were wheat, rice, bananas, sugar, coffee, cocoa, tea, rubber, cotton, jute, wool, iron ore, copper, bauxite, tin (*Year Book of International Trade Statistics*, vol. 2, United Nations, New York, 1982) with the exception of bananas, they all show a high degree of price variation, skew and kurtosis.

11. Further details of this estimator will be found in Hughes Hallett and Ma (1993), together with a range of Monte Carlo tests of its properties. The point to note that the Smith and Spencer estimator has an implicit weighting, which varies over the sample, because they omit the $1/r$ powers. That means each moment gets weighted by the different dimension of units which it brings to the loss function. That penalizes deviations of higher moments from their sample value disproportionately more than equal sized deviations in lower order moments.

12. Numerical simulation studies show the same result: Gemmill, 1985; Hughes Hallett and Ramanujam, 1990; Hughes Hallett, 1991.

REFERENCES

Aitchinson, J. (1963): 'Inverse distributions and independent gamma distributed products of random variables', *Biometrika*, **50**, 505–8.

Brandt, W. and Co-workers (1980): 'North–south: a programme for survival', (London: Pan).

Deaton, A.S. and G. Laroque (1992): 'On the behaviour of commodity prices', *Review of Economic Studies*, **59**, 1–24.

Duffie, D. and K. Singleton (1989): 'Simulated moments estimation of Markov models of asset prices', Discussion paper, Stanford University (Graduate School of Business).

Gemmill, G. (1985): 'Forward contracts or international butter stocks?: a study of their relative efficiencies in stabilising commodity export earnings', *Economic Journal*, **95**, 400–17.

Gilbert, C.L. (1977): 'The post-war tin agreements: an assessment', *Resources Policy*, **3**, 108–17.

—— (1985): 'Futures trading and the welfare evalution of commodity price stabilisation', *Economic Journal*, **95**, 637–61.

—— (1990): 'Primary commodity prices and inflation', *Oxford Review of Economic Policy*, **6**, 77–99.

—— and T. Palaskas (1990): 'Modelling expectations formation in primary commodity markets' in L. Alan Winters and D. Sapsford (ed.), *Primary Commodity Prices: Economic Models and Policy* (Cambridge University Press).

Gregory, A.W. and G.W. Smith (1990): 'Calibration as testing: inference in simulated macroeconomic models', *Econometric Reviews*, **9**, 57–89.

Gustafson, R.L. (1958): 'Carryover levels for grains', US Department of Agriculture, Technical Bulletin 1178, Washington.

Hansen, L.P. (1982): 'Large sample properties of generalised method of moments estimates', *Econometrica*, **50**, 1029–54.

Hughes Hallett, A.J. (1984): 'Optimal stockpiling in a high risk commodity: the case of copper', *Journal of Economic Dynamics and Control*, **8**, 211–38.

—— (1986): 'Commodity market stabilisation and north–south income transfers', *Journal of Development Economics*, **24**, 293–316.

—— (1991): 'Stabilising commodity earnings when there is uncertainty about the price and production distributions', *Journal of Development Studies*, **27**, 26–38.

—— and P. Ramanujam (1990): 'The role of futures markets as stabilisers of commodity earnings', in L. Alan Winters and D. Sapsford (eds), *Primary Commodity Prices: Economic Models and Policy,* (Cambridge University Press and CEPR).

—— and Y. Ma (1993): 'On the accuracy and efficiency of GMM estimators: a Monte Carlo study' in D. Belsley (ed.), *Computational Economics and Econometrics, Vol. 2*, (Boston and Dordrecht: Kluwer).

Johnson, N.L. and S. Kotz (1970): *Continuous Distributions* (New York: Houghton Mifflin).

Kendall, M.G. and A. Stewart (1973): *The Advanced Theory of Statistics*, vol. 2, 3rd edition (London: Griffen).

Moutos, T. and D. Vines (1989): 'North–South macroeconomic interactions: a pedagogic model', *American Economic Review*, papers and proceedings, May 1989.

Smith, G. and M. Spencer (1991): 'Estimation and testing in models of exchange rate target zones and process switching' in P. Krugman and

M. Miller (eds), *Exchange Rate Targets and Currency Bands* (Cambridge University Press and CEPR).

Trevidi, P.K. (1990): 'The prices of perennial crops: the role of expectations and commodity stocks', in L. Alan Winters and D. Sapsford (eds), *Primary Commodity Prices: Economic Models and Policy* (Cambridge University Press).

UNCTAD (1976), 'Integrated programme for commodities', ID/RES/93(IV) (Geneva).

Wright, B. and J. Williams (1982): 'The economic role of commodity storage', *Economic Journal*, **92**, 596–614.

5. Terms of Trade of the South *vis-à-vis* the North: A Macroeconomic Framework

Prabirjit Sarkar

5.1 INTRODUCTION

During 1949–50, Prebisch (1950) and Singer (1950) raised the issue of terms of trade between the underdeveloped and the developed regions (the Periphery and the Centre or the South and the North). At that time, it was mainly the issue of terms of trade between primary products and manufactures. It is now increasingly becoming explicit that the core of the Prebisch–Singer thesis was concerned with the barter and factoral terms of trade between the South and the North (see Sarkar 1986b and 1992b; Sarkar and Singer, 1991; also Sapsford *et al.*, 1992). However, the statistical debate concerning the Prebisch–Singer thesis is more or less concentrated on the terms of trade between primary products and manufactures.

Recently, it has been turned into a hi-tech debate – the latest econometric toolkits are applied to examine the trends and shocks in the terms of trade of primary products (see Cuddington and Urzua, 1989; Powell, 1991; Ardeni and Wright, 1992; Sapsford *et al.*, 1992, etc.). Even Emmanuel (1969) criticized the Prebisch–Singer thesis with the observation:

> ... what worsens is not the terms of trade of certain *products* but those of certain *countries*, regardless of the kind of products they may export or import.

The fact is that this is the essence of the Prebisch–Singer thesis, unknowingly summed up by Emmanuel. The core of the original unequal exchange thesis of Emmanuel (1969) relates not to a deteriorating trend in the terms of trade of the South over a period of time but to the level at which exchanges between the North and the South are taking place at a point of time. The essence of his argument was that the commodity exchange between the North and the South at any point of time is unequal as the difference between the real wages of the two regions is more unequal than what can be accounted for by productivity difference so that the prices of Northern goods in terms of the Southern goods are always higher than the ratio of the amounts of homogeneous labour embodied in them. Granted perfect capital mobility and uniform rate of profit, the double factoral terms of trade between the North and the South is just the ratio of wages in the two regions. But Emmanuel (1969, p. 265) had in mind a widening wage gap, which implies a regular decline in the factoral terms of trade of the South over a period of time. The idea was explicit in Amin (1973) and in the later work of Emmanuel (1979). Then it can be said that the unequal exchange thesis of Emmanuel (1969, 1979) is, in essence, the Prebisch–Singer thesis (Sarkar, 1992a).

Now the question is how to explain the decline in the terms of trade of the South *vis-à-vis* the North. The explanation offered by both Prebisch (1950, 1964) and Singer (1950, 1984) is the asymmetry in the mechanism of distribution of the fruits of technical progress among the producers and the consumers in the North and the South. It was pointed out that 'technical progress in manufacturing industries [of the North] showed in a rise in income while technical progress in the production of food and raw materials in underdeveloped countries [the South] showed in a fall of prices' (Singer, 1950). Therefore, while the prices of Southern exports declined with the improvements in productivity, the export prices of the North did not decline with productivity improvements (Prebisch, 1950, p. 10, Singer, 1950, p. 479). As its evidence, Prebisch (1950, p. 15) cited the case of the USA where during the 40 years preceding the Second World War, manufacturing production costs declined regularly and persistently but the movement of prices did not follow this pattern at all.

An alternative explanation can also be found in the writings of Prebisch and Singer. From the very beginning, Singer (1950, p. 479) considered income inelastic demand for export goods of the

South as an important factor behind the trend-deterioration in the terms of trade of the South. Later on, Prebisch (1951) also joined. Due to the income inelasticity, demand for food and related items expands less than manufactures in the process of growth of the world economy. Moreover, some part of technical progress consists of economies in the use of raw materials (raw material saving technical progress) or development of manufacturing substitutes (e.g. synthetic substitutes) of agricultural products. Spraos (1983) lent support to this explanation.

However, this asymmetry in the responsiveness of demand for exports of the North and South cannot be taken as an adequate explanation. In the first half of the nineteenth century, the classical law, namely, the improvements in the terms of trade of primary products, operated as indicated by the terms-of-trade experience of Britain (see Sarkar, 1986a). In the early days of industrial revolution, fruits of technical progress in the manufacturing industries, particularly in the cotton textile sector, were transmitted to the consumers in the form of fall in prices. Those were days of competitive capitalism as envisaged by the classical writers. At that time, the classical mechanism of distribution of fruits of technical progress was in operation.

The phenomenon of deteriorating terms of trade started in the last quarter of the nineteenth century with the transformation of capitalism in the North by the appearance of monopolies as noted also by Amin (1973, p. 170). This transformation started with the spread of technical progress from traditional manufactures such as cotton textiles towards newer manufactures as noted by Sarkar (1986a,b; 1992a). It seems that changes in the market structures from competition towards monopoly and the consequent changes in the mechanism of distribution of the fruits of technical progress from the classical to the Prebisch–Singer mechanism had played a crucial role in explaining the reversal of the classical law to the Prebisch–Singer observation.

The present paper shows that the diverse mechanism of distribution of the fruits of technical progress due to different market structures in the North and the South can adequately explain the trend–decline in the terms of trade of the South. We don't have to bring in the question of income inelasticity of demand for Southern products. This is important in view of the Sarkar–Singer result that the terms of trade of the South declined not only in the exchange of their primary products for Northern manufactures but also for the exchange of manufactures for manufactures (Sarkar and Singer, 1991, 1993).

In the next section, a simple macroeconomic framework has been presented on the Keynes–Kalecki–Kaldor line. In particular, it is based on an informal model of the world economy presented by Kaldor (1976). Our conclusion is based on this Kaldorian model of the world economy.

5.2 THE MODEL

Throughout the analysis, a fixed exchange rate regime has been assumed. The exchange rate has been set equal to unity. Existence of government budget has been ignored for simplicity. Technology is assumed to be of fixed coefficient type.

The world economy is divided into two regions, the North and the South:

1. The North produces consumers' goods and machines whereas the South produces consumers' goods. Apart from the fact that only the Northern product has consumption and investment uses, there is no other distinguishing feature of the Northern product such as higher income elasticity. It will be assumed that the Northern and Southern products are perfectly complementary in the consumption baskets of the Northern and the Southern consumers so that income elasticity of demand for these two goods is unity.
2. As assumed by Kaldor (1976), the South produces at full capacity so that in response to demand–supply imbalances, price adjusts 'in the classical manner described by Adam Smith' whereas in the North, the greater part of production is concentrated in the hands of large corporations so that the prices are fixed by the producers themselves. A typical producer operates at less than full capacity. Northern prices (in contrast to the prices of South) are not 'market clearing'. The monopoly element in Northern price formation is sought to be captured by Kaleckian mark up pricing rule. The mark up rate (t) fixes the distributive shares of the Northern workers and the capitalists.

3. The capital–output relationship in the South is given by the equation:

$$Y_s = K_s \, q_s \tag{5.1}$$

where the subscript s stands for the South, Y is the level of output, K is the capital stock and q is the (given) gross productivity of capital (including labour productivity) as assumed in Thirlwall (1986).

Due to the existence of surplus capacity, the Northern counterpart of Equation 5.1 is slightly different:

$$Y_n = u_n \, K_n \, q_n \tag{5.2}$$

where the subscript n stands for the North and u is the rate of capacity utilization, <1 in the North (due to the existence of surplus capacity assumed throughout the present analysis).[1]

4. Skipping the details of production and distribution in the South, it is assumed that a constant proportion (s_s) of Southern income is saved.[2] Then the total saving in the South (S_s) is given by the equation:

$$S_s = s_s \, Y_s \tag{5.3}$$

In the North, total profit is assumed to be equal to total saving. Hence, the North also has a proportional saving function as the share of profit, m, is fixed by the given mark up rate $[= 1/(1 + t)]$:

$$S_n = m \, Y_n \tag{5.4}$$

Then the rate of saving to capital stock = the rate of profit. This rate of profit is proportional to the rate of capacity utilization as it is the ratio between profit income and capital stock, $m Y_n / K_n$:

$$r_n = m \, u_n \, q_n \tag{5.5}$$

The G_s line in Figure 5.1 shows this relationship.

5. In the South, the whole of saving is invested on Northern machines. Hence a saving–investment identity holds good:

$$I_s = S_s / P \tag{5.6}$$

where P is the North–South terms of trade (price of Northern goods in terms of Southern goods).[3]

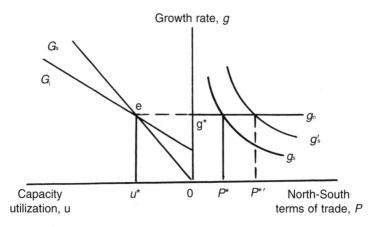

Figure 5.1.   Capital Utilization, Growth and Terms of Trade

In the North, the investment decision is separate from saving
decision. The rate of capital accumulation is assumed to be
directly related to the rate of profit. In linear form, the relationship is:

$$I_n = a + b\, r_n = a + (bmq_n)\, u_n \tag{5.7}$$

As the rate of profit is proportionally related to the rate of
capacity utilization, the rate of capital accumulation is in effect
a direct function of capacity utilization. The G_i line shows this
relationship in Figure 5.1.

6.   The rate of growth of the South (g_s) is an inverse function of
the North–South terms of trade [from Equations 5.1, 5.3 and
5.6]:

$$g_s = q_s\, s_s/P \tag{5.8}$$

Intuitively, it is evident that the higher the price of machines in
terms of Southern goods, the lower the availability of machines
out of a given amount of Southern savings and so the lower
the Southern growth. This inverse relationship is shown by the
line g_s in the right hand quadrant of Figure 5.1.

In the North, the rate of growth is determined by the equality between the rate of saving to capital stock and the rate of
capital accumulation. This is shown by the point of intersection
between the G_s and G_i lines; g^* is the Northern growth rate.

Mathematically, g^* can be derived by equating (5.5) and (5.7) as due to (5.4), the rate of profit is equal to the rate of saving to capital stock:

$$g^* = a/(1 - b) \qquad (5.9)$$

For a meaningful solution, the investment function should have a positive intercept and a less-than-one-type slope ($a > 0$, $b < 1$).

7. On the assumption that the consumption expenditure in the South, $(1 - s_s) Y_s$, is distributed between the Southern and Northern goods in fixed proportions, it follows that a constant proportion of Southern output is exported:

$$Ex_s = [1 - f_s (1 - s_s)] Y_s \qquad (5.10)$$

where Ex_s is the total exports of the South, f_s is the proportion of Southern consumption expenditure made on Southern goods.

Given Equation 5.10, the exports and output of the South grow at the same rate so that the g_s line shows the rate of growth of Southern export supplies to the North.

As the whole of Northern profit income is assumed to be saved, the Northern consumption expenditure equals the Northern wage income. On the assumption that this wage income is allocated between the Southern and Northern goods in fixed proportions, it follows that the Northern growth rate also gives the rate of growth of Northern demand for Southern exports. This is independent of the North–South terms of trade, as shown by the g_n line in the right hand quadrant of Figure 5.1. The point of intersection between the g_s and g_n lines determines the North–South terms of trade, P^*.

Mathematically, the equilibrium solution for the North–South terms of trade can be derived:

$$p^* = (1 - b) s_s q_s / a \qquad (5.11)$$

Given this framework, it can be asked following Findlay (1981): What are the fundamental determinants of the North–South terms of trade? From Equation 5.11, it follows that the fundamental determinants are:

1. The growth rate of the North which is a combination of 'animal spirits' of the Northern investors (parameter a of the

Northern investment function, Equation 5.7) and the responsiveness of Northern investment rate to a change in the rate of profit (parameter b);

2. The factor productivity in the South, q_s; and
3. The saving propensity of the South (s_s) which is an important determinant of the Southern growth rate (along with the Southern productivity, q_s).

Evidently, a rise in factor productivity in the South (q_s) due to a technical progress, is fully reflected in the terms of trade – it turns against the South. Graphically, the g_s line shifts upwards and the North–South terms of trade rises to $p^{*\prime}$. But productivity changes in the North are not reflected in the movements of the terms of trade. Findlay (1980, 1981) arrived at the same conclusion through a different approach. He assumed universal perfect competition. The North was assumed to be a Solow-type economy while the South is a Lewis-type.

Thus it follows that the explanation of the decline in the terms of trade of the South can be found in technical progress and productivity improvements in the South. Irrespective of whether the rate of technical progress and the productivity improvements in the South are higher or lower than that in the North, the South will face a decline in its (barter) terms of trade. Irrespective of whether the South experiences a technical progress or not, any technical progress in the North implies a decline (improvement) in the factoral terms of trade of the South (North) as it is not translated into a lower barter terms of trade for the North. This is 'unequal exchange' which Prebisch (1950), Singer (1950) and Emmanuel (1969, 1979) had in mind.

Thus our simple macroeconomic framework of the world economy shows the theoretical validity of the 'unequal exchange' thesis of Prebisch–Singer and Emmanuel. It just requires the fact that the South has been facing some technical progress along with the North in a long-term setting of the dynamic world. It does not require the presumption that the North has experienced a higher rate of technical progress than the South. The proceeding analysis does not depend on the stylized facts posited by some such as Lewis (1969), namely that the South has experienced a higher rate of technical progress in its export sector relative to its non-traded food sector, unlike the experience of the North (for a formal model, see Evans, 1987).

Recently, Dutt (1988, p. 172) offered an alternative explanation; he showed that a rise in the monopoly power (and an income distribution favouring the Northern capitalists) slows down the rate of growth in the North and leads to a decline in the terms of trade of the South. However, a look at Equation 5.9 shows that our framework finds no support to this conclusion. The fact is that, the conclusion of Dutt (1988) follows specifically from his investment function where both the rate of profit and capacity utilization are taken as two separate variables explaining the rate of capital accumulation. Our framework would support Dutt (1988) if we had his investment function instead of ours:

$$I_n/K_n = a + br_n + cu_n \qquad (5.11)$$
$$(a, b, c > 0)$$

The objection to this type of investment function is that the rate of profit and the rate of capacity utilization are proportionally related as shown in Equation 5.5, given the mark up rate and factor productivity as in Dutt (1988). Hence endogenous variations in the rate of profit come only through changes in the utilization rate. So there is no justification in taking the rate of profit and the utilization rate as two separate explanatory variables.[4]

Thus the explanation offered by Dutt (1988) is not theoretically valid. Darity (1990) also has derived a similar conclusion through a reformulation of Findlay model by introducing a Kaleckian North (and a Lewis type South).

To sum up, the explanation of the long-term decline in the terms of trade of the South lies in the change in the Northern market structures from competition towards monopoly (as noted in Sarkar 1986b; 1992a,b) in a dynamic world of technical progress taking place in both the North and the South. As a result, the classical mechanism of distribution of the fruits of technical progress gave way to the Prebisch–Singer mechanism. Continuous growth in the monopoly power of the Northern capitalists (or the rising mark up rate in Northern manufacturing) may or may not be a fact; but this is not needed to explain the terms of trade decline.[5]

NOTES

1. In an oligopolistic market structure, surplus capacity always exists. A number

of justifications for the existence of surplus capacity can be provided – 'building capacity ahead of demand' to 'provide a margin of safety against a sudden upswing in sales, maintaining barriers to entry' etc. (Taylor, 1985).

2. This leaves room for alternative specifications of the South. There may exist a national government that mobilizes resources for investment. Hence the assumption of saving-investment identity (made later) may be justified.

3. Due to this saving-investment identity, the value of Southern exports equals the value of Southern imports for consumption and investment of Northern goods. Thus capital flows and issues of debt are ignored.

4. There is a lot of ambiguities in the relationship between distribution and growth as shown by Blecker (1989), Bhaduri and Marglin (1990) and Sarkar (1992c; 1993a,b).

5. As a by-product, this framework can be used to question the theoretical validity of the export-led growth strategy for the South as a whole. Stepping up the rate of growth of Southern exports required a higher rate of growth of Southern output. This leads to a fall in the terms of trade of the South.

REFERENCES

Amin, S. (1973): *Unequal Development*, (Eng. translation, 1976), (Delhi: Oxford University Press).

Ardeni, P.G. and B. Wright (1992): 'The Prebisch–Singer hypothesis: a reappraisal independent of stationarity hypothesis', *The Economic Journal*, **102** (413), 803–12.

Bhaduri, A. and M. Marglin (1990): 'Unemployment and the real wage: the economic basis for contesting political ideologies', *Cambridge Journal of Economics*, **14**, 375–93.

Blecker, R.A. (1989): International competition, income distribution and economic growth', *Cambridge Journal of Economics*, **13**, 395–412.

Cuddington, J.T. and C.M. Urzua (1989): 'Trends and cycles in the net barter terms of trade: a new approach', *The Economic Journal*, **99**, 426–42.

Darity, W. Jr. (1990): 'The fundamental determinants of the terms of trade reconsidered: long-run and long-period equilibrium', *The Economic Journal*, **80**, 816–27.

Dutt, A.K. (1988): 'Monopoly power and uneven development: Baran revisited', *Journal of Development Studies*, **24**, 161–76.

Emmanuel, A. (1969): *Unequal Exchange* (Eng. translation, 1972), (New York: Monthly Review Press).

—— (1979): 'The dynamics of unequal exchange/unequal development', paper presented to a conference on Dependence at the London School of Economics.

Evans, D. (1987): 'The long-run determinants of North–South terms of trade and some recent empirical evidence', *World Development*, **15**, 657–72.

Findlay, R. (1980): 'The terms of trade and equilibrium growth in the world economy', *American Economic Review*, **70**, 291–9.

—— (1981): 'The fundamental determinants of the terms of trade', in S. Grassman and E. Lundberg (eds), *The World Economic Order*, (London: Macmillan), 425–57.

Kaldor, N. (1976): 'Inflation and recession in the world economy', *The Economic Journal*, **86**, 703–14.

Kalecki, M. (1971): *Selected Essays in the Dynamics of the Capitalist Economy*, (Cambridge University Press).

Lewis, W.A. (1969): *Aspects of Tropical Trade, 1883–1965*, Stockholm: Alnquist and Wickshell.

Powell, A. (1991): 'Commodity and developing country terms of trade: what does the long-run show?' *The Economic Journal*, **101** (409), 1485–96.

Prebisch, R. (1950): *The Economic Development of Latin America and its Principal Problems* (New York: United Nations).

—— (1951): 'The spread of technical progress and the terms of trade', in the UN, *Economic Survey of Latin America* (1949), (New York: UN Department of Economic Affairs).

—— (1964): *Towards a New Trade Policy for Development*, New York: United Nations for UNCTAD.

Sapsford, D., Sarkar, P. and Singer, H.W. (1992): 'The Prebisch–Singer terms of trade controversy revisited', *Journal of International Development*, **4**, 315–332.

Sarkar, Prabirjit (1986a): 'The terms of trade experience of Britian since the nineteenth century', *Journal of Development Studies*, **23** (1), 20–39.

—— (1986b): 'The Singer–Prebisch hypothesis: a statistical evaluation', *Cambridge Journal of Economics*, **10**, 355–71.

—— (1992a): 'Political economy of terms of trade between the North and the South', in Helena Lindholm (ed.), *Approaches to the Study of International Political Economy*, (Gothenberg University, Sweden: PADRIGU).

—— (1992b): 'Terms of trade of the South *vis-à-vis* the North: are they declining?', *IDS Discussion Paper*, no 304, Sussex: IDS.

—— (1992c): 'Industrial growth and income inequality: an examination of 'stagnationism' with special reference to India', *Journal of Quantitative Economics*, **8**, 125–38.

—— (1993a): 'Distribution and growth: a critical note on "stagnationism"', *Review of Radical Political Economics*, **25**, 62–70.

—— (1993b): 'Effective demand and income distribution in the context of agriculture–industry demand linkage: a two-sector macroeconomic framework', *Journal of Macroeconomics*, **15**, Fall, 787–803.

Sarkar, Prabirjit and H.W. Singer (1991): 'Manufactured exports of developing countries and their terms of trade since 1965', *World Development*, **19**, 333–40.

—— (1993): 'Manufacture – manufacture terms of trade deterioration: a reply', *World Development*, **21**, 1617–20.

Singer, H.W. (1950): 'The distribution of gains between investing and borrowing countries', *American Economic Review*, **40**, 473–85.

—— (1984): 'Terms of trade controversy and the evolution of soft financing: early years in the UN: 1947–1951', in M. Meier and D. Seers (eds), *Pioneers in Development*, (Oxford University Press).

—— (1987): 'Terms of trade and economic development', in J. Eatwell, M. Milgate and P. Newman (eds), *The New Palgrave: a Dictionary of Economics*, (London: Macmillan), 626–8.

Spraos, J. (1983): *Inequalising Trade?*, (Oxford: Clarendon Press).

Taylor, L. (1985): 'A stagnationist model of economic growth', *Cambridge Journal of Economics*, **9**, 383–403.

Thirlwall, A.P. (1986): 'A general model of growth and development on Kaldorian lines', *Oxford Economic Papers*, **38**, 199–219.

6. Trend and Volatility in the Terms of Trade: Consequences for Growth

H.W. Singer and Matthias Lutz

6.1 INTRODUCTION

Section 6.2 of this paper deals mainly with terms of trade volatility – a neglected aspect of the terms of trade debate. Volatility is related to uncertainty. The greater the degree of volatility, the greater are the year-to-year fluctuations, and hence the greater the average forecast error made by the economic agents concerned. It is in this sense that the effect of volatility on the economy can be considered a separate factor from the more widely discussed terms of trade trend effects.

The first part therefore places volatility into the wider context of the effects of the terms of trade on output growth. Several channels are discussed through which volatility affects growth. There follows a longer discussion and interpretation of some recent results from a panel estimation examining the effects of volatility – using a simple measure of year-to-year change – on growth in a large sample of countries.

The empirical analysis undertaken specifically for this paper can be found in Section 6.3. It is a cross-section analysis employing a standard neoclassical production function approach, augmented by the trend and volatility components of the terms of trade. The principal measure of volatility used is the estimated standard deviation of the residuals in a regression of the terms of trade (in logs) on a trend variable.

After a closer analysis of the relationships between the estimated trends and volatilities of both net barter and income terms of trade, a number of regressions are estimated to look at the overall effects of the variables in question on growth. What follows is a detailed examination of the question whether the effects of terms of trade trends and volatility on growth differ between countries according to their economic characteristics. Section 6.4 provides a brief set of conclusions.

6.2   TERMS OF TRADE VOLATILITY: AN OVERVIEW

The question of volatility of terms of trade as distinct from trends is paralleled by the discussion in the literature of instability in commodity prices and export earnings as distinct from their trend. However, while in the case of commodity prices at least as much, if not more, attention has been paid to the problem of instability than of trend, the opposite is the case in terms of trade. Here, work on trends – both theoretical and empirical – has far outweighed work on instability or volatility. In fact the latter has hardly been discussed until very recently (Edström and Singer, 1992).

Although discussion of volatility or instability has almost exclusively concentrated on commodity prices, export unit values or export earnings, rather than terms of trade, in some sense it is the latter that seems the more important and more relevant. Obviously, if instability of commodity prices or export unit values is accompanied by similar instability in prices of manufactured goods or import unit values in the same direction (i.e. if the two tend to fluctuate pro-cyclically), the impact on terms of trade and on the economies of the countries concerned will be neutralized or greatly mitigated. What matters to them are the terms of trade rather than the unit values of their exports. So why not go directly to terms of trade and try to measure their fluctuations and their impact on the economy of countries?

The presumption – as in the case of commodity prices or export unit values – is that volatility is a bad thing. It may be presumed to increase the risks of investment and hence reduce the incentive and volume of investment; to disrupt development plans, including structural adjustment programmes; to result in price instability and price distortions with a tendency towards inflation; to disrupt normal price relationships between the traded and non-traded sectors; to destabilize domestic incomes; and as an overall result to reduce growth. This is the starting hypothesis that we examine in this paper. In the case of commodity prices and export unit values as well as export earnings, this presumption – although it sounds very persuasive – has not been clearly supported by empirical studies. While some authors have supported it, others (working with different data, time periods, and countries) have questioned it, and have in fact identified beneficial effects of instability (Maizels, 1992). As will be seen, some of our results also serve to question the negative effects of instability.

Beyond the impact of instability of commodity prices and export earnings on the individual countries concerned leading economists, prominently among them Keynes and Kaldor, have argued that this instability has a harmful effect also on the world economy as a whole, that it intensifies trade cycles and has a deflationary and growth-retarding impact overall (Hart, Kaldor and Tinbergen, 1964). The current paper has a much more modest scope. We are not trying to test the Keynes–Kaldor thesis that this instability is harmful to stable exchange rates and world economic growth. However, we wish to express a belief that the Keynes–Kaldor line of thinking and the related suggestions for international buffer stocks and/or commodity-based currency arrangements do not deserve the criticism and neglect that they suffer in the current neo-liberal era. In particular, we wish to agree with the view expressed by Alf Maizels that the deterioration of terms of trade as well as their instability, have led to circular and cumulative harmful effects on the developed as well as the developing countries.

Although the study of instability or volatility of terms of trade is of interest as such, clearly special interest must attach to the effects of downward volatility of major dimensions, the 'terms of trade shocks'. In the case of upward volatility of major dimensions, i.e. pleasant terms of trade surprises, we would expect any negative impact of volatility to cancel out, or at least partially cancel out, with the positive effect of the improvement in terms of trade; whereas in the case of downward shocks the negative effect of volatility would be further accentuated by the negative effect of the deterioration in terms of trade, possibly with cumulative and dynamically interacting effect. Such commonsense expectations were, however, not clearly confirmed by such statistical analyses as we were able to undertake. One of the reasons may be that in the case of upward shocks or 'pleasant surprises' there is always a danger of Dutch Disease – a fact well known from the experience of oil exporters.

Our initial statistical analyses were based on the method of pooled data. By recording and correlating year-to-year movements of terms of trade over a large number of years and for a large number of countries we were able to obtain a great mass of data so that even relatively slight or flat or confused degrees of correlation acquire additional significance from the large number of observations. The method and results obtained are described in more detail by Edström and Singer (1992) and were further developed by the same two authors in a presentation to the DSA meeting in Nottingham, September 1992. A first summary of the results obtained is shown in Table 6.1.

The result is not unexpected. The 20 countries with the most stable terms of trade show higher income growth over the 19-year period covered than the 20 countries with the most volatile terms of trade. Moreover, the difference is not inconsiderable – the 20 most stable countries experienced GNP growth almost 0.8 per cent higher than that of the most volatile countries. In relative terms their GNP grew over 20 per cent faster than the most volatile countries. Over a long period, such as the 18 years reviewed, such differ-

Table 6.1   Annual % changes (and fluctuations) averaged over the years 1970–88 in 79 non-oil countries

No.	Country group	GNP growth	TT variability	TT trend change
		(% p.a.)	(%)	(% p.a.)
79	All non-oil (average)	(3.57)	(9.42)	(–0.54)
20	Fastest GNP growth	6.14	9.63	–0.10
20	Slowest GNP growth	1.36	10.10	–0.75
20	Most stable TT	3.98	4.76	–0.72
20	Most volatile TT	3.21	15.45	0.43
20	Best TT improvement	3.87	12.96	1.43
20	Worst TT decline	3.36	9.16	–2.34

ences accumulate into a considerable divergence (about 18 per cent). It should be noted that these results relate to non-oil countries only – for oil-exporting countries the results of the two big jumps in oil prices in 1973 and 1979 would show up in even sharper increases in GNP growth.

The negative correlation between terms of trade volatility and GNP growth is confirmed by the multiple correlation analysis relating to all 79 countries. With GNP growth as the dependent variable and both trends and volatility in terms of trade as independent variables, the volatility factor has clearly significant negative correlation with GNP growth (with a T-ratio of –3.285, significant at the 0.001 level).[1]

The negative relationship between terms of trade instability and GNP growth is further confirmed by the fact that the 20 fastest-growing countries have lower variability than the 20 slowest-growing countries, although the difference is not great.

Another result which is perhaps somewhat more surprising is that the 20 most stable countries showed a declining trend in terms of trade over the period to the extent of 0.7 per cent, while the 20 most volatile countries showed a positive trend in their terms of trade to the extent of 0.4 per cent. This finding, i.e. that declining terms of trade tend to be associated with greater stability, and vice versa, is also confirmed by the multiple regression analysis applied to our whole sample of 79 countries.

This introduces something of a compensatory or mitigating feature into the picture: there is a tendency for the negative (positive) impact of high (low) volatility to be compensated by the opposite positive (negative) effect of improving (deteriorating) terms of trade. This compensatory feature is confirmed by the fact that the 20 countries with the best terms of trade improvement have higher instability than the countries with the worst terms of trade decline.

The introduction of volatility as a second independent variable improves the explanatory power of trend in terms of trade alone as a determinant of GNP growth. The coefficient of determination (r^2) of 11.3 per cent may not seem particularly impressive, but then clearly GNP growth is the result of a combination of a great multitude of factors including the quality of domestic policies, the weather, growth in the world economy, rate of investment, literacy, health, etc.

We have also experimented with time lags in the correlation of GNP growth with volatility, on the assumption that the effect on GNP growth may be delayed by a year or two, but the results have been rather inconclusive. There seems no strong tendency for delayed effects or for cumulative effects in subsequent years. It is, however, the case that on our calculations an initial 30 per cent decline in terms of trade will result in an initial reduction in the rate of growth of 1.5 per cent which will be extended to a loss of over 2 per cent in the subsequent year before stabilizing. By contrast a 30 per cent improvement will also result in an initial drop in GNP growth (the effect of the shock outweighing the fact of improvement), but there will be a recovery in the next year beyond the initial growth rate with subsequent stabilization. The initial drop in GNP growth may be surprising but sudden and unexpected improvements are not easily and quickly channelled into growth and one year is not a long period for the favourable trend change to overcome the immediate disruptive shock effect.

The results reported so far seem to be reasonably clear and plausible – but there is a potential snag. The measure of volatility (or variability or instability – these terms have been used as interchangeable) on which these results are based are the log of the simple year-to-year changes in terms of trade regardless of sign. This can be defended on the grounds that this is what really matters to countries. The year-to-year change, apart from the fact that there is economic reality behind it, also has the statistical advantage – already mentioned – that it helps to give us a great mass of data that improves the significance of any findings. But it should be clear that statistically or logically this is not an ideal measure of volatility. The year-to-year change obviously includes an element of trend in terms of trade as well as volatility (unless the trend is completely flat). If the terms of trade improve or deteriorate from one year to another by say, 5 per cent, some of this will be part of a trend and some of it will be volatility, if the trend is also positive. If the terms of trade trend goes in the opposite direction from the year-to-year change the actual volatility will be greater than the year-to-year change indicates, and vice versa. When a country experiences a 5 per cent improvement or deterioration from one year to the next, it does not make any immediate difference to the country whether this is trend or volatility or a mixture of both. It does, however, make some difference in deciding whether to treat the change as sustainable or not, and hence in policies to deal with it. Furthermore, given the predominance of declining terms of trade trends, we cannot be sure that the negative impact of our instability measure on growth is not partly simply again the impact of terms of trade trends (which all measures agree are positively correlated with GNP growth).

For these reasons we have experimented with other measures of volatility that are statistically less objectionable. The most obvious of such alternative measures is the standard deviation from trend, but we have also tested the average absolute deviation from the regression line, the square of the average deviation from the regression line (giving extra weight to large deviations) and deviation as a percentage of the trend line, etc. All these measures turned out to be very closely correlated amongst each other, with r^2 of the order of 0.8 to 0.9. Presumably the standard deviation from the regression line would be the best measure. Using this measure, no clear or statistically significant relationship between variability and GNP growth could be established. If anything, the impact turned out to be positive for the low-income countries in the sample. This lends some support to the compensatory element mentioned above, due to the fact that there was some tendency for high volatility to occur in combination with rising terms of trade trends.

The discussion so far has been related to barter terms of trade. In some ways, of course, it is instability in income terms of trade, or capacity to import, which matters more. We have calculated the correlation in volatility between barter terms of trade and income terms of trade and found it fairly strong ($r^2 = 62$ per cent). This seems to show that changes in export volumes (which constitute the difference between income terms of trade and barter terms of trade) have some influence but do not effectively counteract the impact of volatility in barter terms of trade. On the other hand, the correlation between trends in barter terms of trade and income terms of trade (as distinct from their volatility) is quite loose ($r^2 = 24$ per cent). Thus, as far as trends are concerned, volume of exports is of great importance compared with price trends. This will be particularly true of countries that manage to diversify their exports into processed commodities and manufactures. Diversification into manufactures does not necessarily change price trends very much, but it does have a decisive influence in improving income terms of trade (Sarkar and Singer, 1991).

In our full sample (including oil exporters and developed countries) the average trend was –1.7 per cent p.a. and average volatility (now measured as the standard deviation from trend) was 14.7 per cent. This means that average volatility was 8 to 9 times larger than the annual trend so that it would take 8 to 9 years on average for trends to become dominant over fluctuation. This would then seem to be the dividing point between the shorter period in which volatility is the more important problem and the longer period in which trend is dominant.

For income terms of trade the trend value was +3.9 per cent p.a. and average volatility was 18.0 per cent. In this case, average volatility was only 4 to 5 times higher than annual trend, and the shorter volatility-dominated period was only 4 to 5 years. However, if the income terms of trade are calculated on a per capita basis, i.e. corrected for the increase in population (as they should be since they are supposed to measure capacity to import), the growth trend of income terms of trade is reduced from +3.9 per cent to +2.2 per cent, and the volatility of 18 per cent represents more or less the same ratio of 8 to 9 times the trend as in the case of barter terms of trade.

It may be noted that volatility for income terms of trade at 18.0 per cent is higher than for barter terms of trade at 14.7 per cent. This means that the volume of exports (which is the difference between income terms of trade and barter terms of trade) contributes to volatility. While it serves to remedy and reverse the declining trend in barter terms of trade it does so at the cost of increasing volatility.

The income terms of trade are supposed to measure capacity to import, but under present circumstances this meaning has become somewhat doubtful. Most developing countries – practically all with the exception of some oil exporters – are heavily indebted so that the income terms of trade measure the capacity of servicing debt rather than capacity to import. Moreover, the fact that the volume of exports of developing countries has considerably increased, converting negative trends in barter terms of trade into positive trends of income terms of trade even on a per capita basis, raises problems of its own. The increase in the volume of exports is not costless; it absorbs domestic resources away from consumption or domestic investment and it is also not costless in terms of foreign exchange as a result of imported inputs into exports. The clearest case is that of export cash crops competing with food for domestic consumption.

Our sample reveals a tendency for volatility in barter terms of trade to be higher in low-income countries and to be negatively correlated with per capita income levels. The volatility (average standard deviation) was 16 per cent for low-income countries, 15 per cent for middle-income countries and 12 per cent for high-income countries. This result is plausible since the higher income countries have more diversified exports. It adds to the seriousness of the volatility problem: volatility is highest among those countries least able to cope with its consequences. Similarly, for the income terms of trade, volatility was 21 per cent for low-income countries, 20 per cent for middle-income countries and 10 per cent for high-income countries. It may be noted that in the low- and middle-income countries fluctuations in the volume of exports add to the volatility of barter terms of trade, whereas in the high-income countries they act in a compensatory manner and reduce volatility.

6.3 TERMS OF TRADE TREND AND VOLATILITY: AN EMPIRICAL ANALYSIS

Our empirical analysis consists of a cross-section study which uses an 'augmented' production function approach, where the extra terms in the regression equations are the trend in the terms of trade and a measure of their volatility. The assumed model under investigation is:

$$Y = Y(K, L, t, v) \qquad (6.1)$$

where Y, K and L are the familiar output, capital and labour, and t and v are the terms of trade trend and volatility. The reasons for the inclusion of the latter two variables have been explained in Section 6.2. In brief, the trend can be regarded as the secular change in the terms of trade, whereas the volatility variable captures the extent of unexpected changes in the terms of trade. It is in this sense that the two variables can be expected to affect output growth through separate channels.

The first issue thus concerns the derivation of the trend and volatility components in the terms of trade. This problem is closely related to the distinction between the permanent and cyclical components in any given non-stationary time series. In the recent past a large body of literature has examined the correct representation of the trend component, and in particular the question whether macroeconomic time-series contain a unit root (for a recent review see Campbell and Perron, 1991). Unfortunately, unit root tests against trend-stationary alternatives can be fairly problematic. Not only is there near-observational equivalence, but these tests often have very low power, particularly in samples with less than 50 observations (DeJong *et al.*, 1992).

The sample[2] examined in this paper contains only 21 observations per country. For this reason, the approach chosen here is fairly simple, but held to provide a useful approximation to the 'true' model. It involves the regression of each country's terms of trade series on a constant and a linear time trend:

$$x_t = \beta_0 + \beta_1 \text{ trend} + u_t \qquad (6.2)$$

where x_t is the natural logarithm of the terms of trade variable (net barter or income terms of trade), trend is the linear time trend $(1, 2, 3 \ldots, T)$ and u_t the series of estimated residuals.

The estimated coefficient on the time trend, β_1, is then taken as the estimate of the trend τ in the terms of trade over the sample period considered[3]. It can be interpreted as the average growth rate of the terms of trade over the sample period. The most intuitive measure of volatility is the estimated standard error from that regression, i.e. the estimated standard deviation of the residuals from the trend line. This will be our principal measure of volatility, and from now on noted as v_1.

Let us first look at these estimated trends and volatilities (v_1), both for the net barter terms of trade (NBTT) and the income terms of trade (ITT). Table 6.2 provides a summary of these estimates for the total sample and a variety of subcategories. For the NBTT, it can be observed that there has been an overall deterioration in the terms of trade trend for the countries in the sample[4]. It appears that low income countries – heavily concentrated in Sub-Saharan Africa – have fared slightly worse than the richer countries, although this depends to some degree on how they are classified. The oil-exporting countries are the only ones that have achieved an overall improvement in the terms of trade. Non-fuel primary-product exporters are those that have fared worst. In this

Table 6.2 Estimated trends and volatilities (1968–88)

	Net barter terms of trade			Income terms of trade			Correlation coefficients: NBTT & ITT	
	Trend	Volatility	Corr. coeff.[d]	Trend	Volatility	Corr. coeff.	Trend	Volatility
All countries (st.dev.)	-0.017 (0.025)	0.147 (0.084)	0.559	0.039 (0.044)	0.180 (0.111)	0.131	0.240	0.617
OECD	-0.023	0.106	0.514	0.048	0.091	0.500	-0.124	0.237
LDCs	-0.015	0.160	0.597	0.036	0.207	0.196	0.265	0.601
Sub-Sah. Africa	-0.020	0.166	0.533	0.016	0.204	0.192	0.140	0.785
Low income Cs[a]	-0.020	0.160	0.459	0.014	0.208	0.331	0.421	0.735
Middle income Cs	-0.016	0.152	0.563	0.050	0.203	0.089	0.001	0.378
High income Cs	-0.015	0.122	0.749	0.051	0.096	0.551	0.516	0.915
Oil exporters	0.015	0.264	0.794	0.070	0.322	0.137	0.296	0.636
Manuf. exporters	-0.017	0.100	-0.410	0.046	0.041	0.107	0.085	-0.120
Pr. pr. exps	-0.025	0.140	0.000	0.027	0.176	-0.027	0.039	0.260

Table 6.2 Estimated trends and volatilities (1968–88) (continued)

	Net barter terms of trade			Income terms of trade			Correlation coefficients NBTT & ITT	
	Trend	Volatility	Corr. coeff.[d]	Trend	Volatility	Corr. coeff.	Trend	Volatility
LDC oil exporters	0.020	0.279	0.781	0.072	0.340	0.008	0.243	0.574
LDC manuf. exps[b]	-0.018	0.103	-0.556	0.058	0.172	0.452	-0.015	-0.379
LDC pr. pr. exps	-0.025	0.144	-0.013	0.024	0.179	-0.039	0.050	0.238
Small countries[c]	-0.018	0.145	0.451	0.035	0.188	0.076	0.283	0.558
Medium countries	-0.016	0.146	0.648	0.034	0.161	0.067	0.086	0.642
Large countries	-0.014	0.157	0.717	0.058	0.189	0.397	0.352	0.772

Notes:
(a) Following the classification in the 1990 World Development Report.
(b) Manufacturing exporters are those whose average ratio of manufacturing to total exports over the 1968–88 period exceeds 30%.
    Primary product exporters are those where the non-oil primary products exports are on average greater than 50% of total exports over the same period.
(c) Small countries: population < 10 million in 1988. Medium countries: population between 10 and 50 million in 1988. Large countries: population > 50 million in 1988.
(d) The correlation coefficient between trend and volatility, where volatility is the estimated standard error from the trend equation.

last respect there seems little difference between LDCs and the industrialized countries.

Volatility in the NBTT has been by far greatest in the oil-exporting countries. There is also some evidence, though not statistically significant[5], that low-income countries have had to deal with greater volatility in their NBTT; this is to some degree due to the fact that most oil-exporters are LDCs. The least affected have been those that relied mainly on manufacturing exports, regardless of whether they are developed or developing countries. Clearly the concentration of manufacturing exporters among the OECD countries helps to explain the low degree of volatility in their NBTT.

Arguably of even greater importance for economic growth than the NBTT are the income terms of trade, which provide a measure of the capacity to import[6]. Here the differences between low-income and the other countries are more marked. Low-income countries have only experienced an average annual growth rate of 1.4 per cent in their capacity to import during the sample period (practically equal to zero on a per capita basis). This compares with an average of around 5 per cent for both the OECD and the group of middle-income countries. The difference is statistically significant, with t-ratios of 3.28 (compared to high-income countries) and 3.10 (compared to middle-income countries)[7]. Similarly, low-income countries have experienced greater levels of volatility in their ITT (partly due to the concentration of oil-exporting countries, who faced the worst fluctuations of all, among them). Equality of volatility measures between low-income and middle/high-income countries can also be rejected statistically.

The relatively low trend in the income terms of trade can only partly be explained by the slightly more negative trend in the NBTT found in these countries. The correlation coefficient between the two trend values is 0.411. An alternative explanation might be the higher level of terms of trade volatility the poorer countries had to deal with, and its possible negative effect on export volume. However, this line of reasoning is not the full explanation, as shown by the middle-income countries who faced a similarly negative trend in the NBTT, but achieved a much greater trend growth rate in the ITT.

Table 6.1 also reports the correlation coefficients between the trend in the two terms of trade measures, the two volatilities and between trend and volatility. Overall, there is only a loose correspondence between the two terms of trade trends, indicating that the ITT trend was to a considerable part determined by export volumes in the sample countries. The ITT volatility, on the other hand, seems to be fairly closely related to the volatility in the NBTT (with the exception of manufacturing exporters). This suggests that changes in the NBTT had a relatively bigger impact on short run fluctuations in export earnings than on their long-term trend.

The overall correlation coefficients between trend and volatility are positive for both terms of trade variables, though the NBTT exhibit a much closer correlation between trend and volatility. This implies that positive trends have to be associated with greater volatility. A major reason for this relationship is the oil-exporting countries. Looking at manufacturing and non-fuel primary-product producers separately, the relationship is either reversed or fails to exist (for the NBTT).

One may also learn something from a closer look at trends and volatilities in the terms of trade in individual countries. In particular, one might want to know if there are any 'outliers', i.e. countries that are significantly different from the rest. Figure 6.1 and Figure 6.2 provide scatter-plots of trend and volatility for each country. The axes in both figures do not intersect at the origin, but at the mean across the entire sample for each variable. This provides a better overview of relative performances. Names are attached to the most extreme outliers.

The statistical criterion chosen to select significant outliers is that their distance from the mean has to be greater than 1.5 times the standard deviation[8]. For the NBTT this implies that an outlier has to lie outside the interval [−0.054, 0.022] for the trend, and [0.222, 0.273] for the volatility measure. For the ITT, the respective intervals are [−0.028, 0.105], and [0.013, 0.347].

There are five countries whose NBTT trend can be deemed to be a positive outlier (Algeria: 0.072, Gabon: 0.053, Indonesia: 0.061, Kuwait: 0.104, and Nigeria: 0.047) – all oil-exporters. The two negative outliers are Chile (−0.062) and Zambia (−0.074), both of whom have suffered from a large fall in the price of their main export commodity – copper. With respect to NBTT volatility, there are seven outliers (Algeria: 0.452, Ecuador: 0.327, Fiji: 0.283, Gabon: 0.322, Indonesia: 0.296, Kuwait: 0.481 and Nigeria: 0.495), all but one of whom are, again, oil-exporters.

The ITT outliers present a somewhat different picture. The only similarity is that the volatility outliers are again mainly oil-exporters

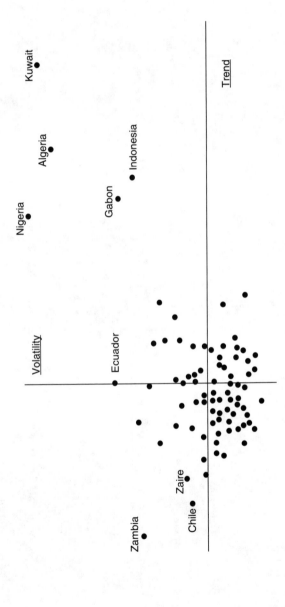

Note: The axes meet at the respective sample means (Trend: −0.017; Volatility: 0.147).

Figure 6.1 Net barter terms of trade – trend and volatility

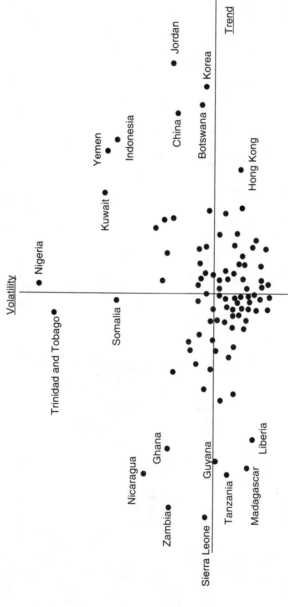

Note: The axes meet at the respective sample means (Trend: 0.039; Volatility: 0.180).

Figure 6.2 *Income terms of trade – trend and volatility*

(Indonesia: 0.438, Kuwait: 0.462, Nicaragua: 0.353, Nigeria: 0.628, Somalia: 0.426, Trinidad and Tobago: 0.584, Yemen: 0.457), although several of the countries experiencing unusually large fluctuations in their NBTT somehow seemed to have managed to stabilize their ITT through their export supply behaviour. The seven positive outliers with respect to the trend in their ITT contain several of the star performers of the past decades (Botswana: 0.141, China: 0.136, Hong Kong: 0.106, Indonesia: 0.122, Jordan: 0.164, Korea: 0.152, Yemen: 0.115). This implies not only that these countries have disproportionately expanded their export volumes but also that most oil-exporters did not manage to convert the large NBTT gains into equivalent increases in their ITT.

The most striking feature of the group of countries that saw particularly large falls in their ITT is that three-quarters are Sub-Saharan African countries (Ghana: −0.045, Guyana: −0.051, Liberia: −0.040, Madagascar: −0.055, Nicaragua: −0.058, Sierra Leone: −0.082, Tanzania: −0.059, Zambia: −0.077). Only in the case of Zambia can this mainly be attributed to a strongly negative trend in the NBTT. This evidence suggests that the above countries – compared to the overall sample – had significant problems in maintaining an adequate volume of exports.

Before moving to the econometric analysis and discussion of regression results, it should be noted that the standard error of the deviations from the trend line, v_1, is not the only possible measure of volatility. In order not to narrow the subsequent analysis unduly, three alternative measures of volatility will be used as explanatory variables. These are:

$$v_2 = \frac{1}{T} \sum_{t=1}^{T} \frac{\left| \Pi_t - \hat{\Pi}_t \right|}{\hat{\Pi}_t}$$

$$v_3 = \frac{1}{T} \sum_{t=1}^{T} \left(\log \Pi_t - \log \hat{\Pi}_t \right)^2$$

$$v_4 = \frac{100}{\overline{\Pi}} \sum_{t=2}^{T} \frac{\left| \log \Pi_t - \log \Pi_{t-1} - \beta_2 \right|}{T-1}$$

where Π_t = terms of trade index at time t, and $\hat{}$ indicates a fitted value.

The first alternative measure, v_2, is the average absolute deviation from the estimated regression line. The second, v_3, is the squared average deviation from the regression line, and thus gives greater weight to larger deviations. The third measure, v_4, gives the average deviation of the actual growth rate in the terms of trade from the estimated trend coefficient, as a percentage of the average terms of trade[9]. That all four measures of volatility are closely related is shown in Table 6.3 which shows their estimated correlation coefficients.

Let us now move to the regressions. The regression equations are typical cross-section production functions, the dependent variable being average real output growth during the sample period, with added terms of trade trend and volatility variables. Several specifications were estimated, all of which contain the average investment/GDP ratio (proxying the rate of growth of capital), and the average population growth rate (as a proxy for labour force growth) over the sample period[10]. Four specifications contain intercept and interactive dummy variables allowing for the estimation of the coefficients of interest for a number of subgroups. The six specifications are:

1. $y = \Omega + u$
2. $y = \Omega + \Theta + u$
3. $y = \Omega + \Theta + \gamma_1 D_L + \gamma_2 D_H + \gamma_3 \tau_L + \gamma_4 \tau_H + \gamma_5 v_L + \gamma_6 v_H + u$
4. $y = \Omega + \Theta + \gamma_1 D_{SSA} + \gamma_2 D_{LA} + \gamma_3 \tau_{SSA} + \gamma_4 \tau_{LA} + \gamma_5 v_{SSA} + \gamma_6 v_{LA}$
   $+ u$
5. $y = \Omega + \Theta + \gamma_1 D_{OIL} + \gamma_2 D_{MAN} + \gamma_3 \tau_{OIL} + \gamma_4 \tau_{MAN} + \gamma_5 v_{OIL}$
   $+ \gamma_6 v_{MAN} + u$
6. $y = \Omega + \Theta + \gamma_1 D_{DO} + \gamma_2 D_{DM} + \gamma_3 D_{DPP} + \gamma_4 \tau_{DO} + \gamma_5 \tau_{DM} + \gamma_6 \tau_{DPP}$
   $+ \gamma_7 v_{DO} + \gamma_8 v_{DM} + \gamma_9 v_{DPP} + u$

Table 6.3   Estimated correlation coefficients – four measures of volatility

	Net Barter Terms of Trade				Income Terms of Trade		
	v_2	v_3	v_4		v_2	v_3	v_4
v_1	0.983	0.920	0.913	v_1	0.983	0.885	0.878
v_2		0.960	0.851	v_2		0.938	0.851
v_3			0.797	v_3			0.740

Note: The measures are explained in the text.

where: $\Omega = (\beta_0 + \beta_1\ I/Y + \beta_2\ gpop)$
$\Theta = (\beta_3\tau + \beta_4 v)$

and: gyq = [arithm.] Average annual GDP growth rate (1968–88);

I/Y = [arithm.] Average annual investment/GDP ratio (1968–88);

gpop = [arithm.] Average annual population growth rate (1968–88);

τ = Estimated trend in the terms of trade;

v = Estimated volatility in the terms of trade;

τ_i, v_i = Interactive dummies for the relevant subgroup (= τ, v for countries in subgroup, 0 otherwise)

D_i = Intercept dummy for relevant subgroup (=1 for the countries in subgroup, 0 otherwise);

and the subscripts denote the following subgroupings:

L = Low-income countries;
H = High-income countries;
SSA = Sub-Saharan African countries;
LA = Latin-American countries;
OIL = Oil exporters;
MAN = Manufactured goods exporters;
DO = LDC oil exporters;
DM = LDC manufactured goods exporters;
DPP = LDC primary product exporters.

In those regressions with interactive dummy variables (3–6), the coefficient on the interactive dummy tells us whether (if statistically significant), and how different the particular subgroup is from the 'control' group. To obtain the actual responsiveness of the subgroup's output growth rate to the particular variable in question, the coefficient on the interactive dummy must be added to the overall coefficient. For instance, to obtain the actual coefficient for the terms of trade trend τ for Sub-Saharan African countries in Specification 4, γ_4 must be added to β_4. With respect to the interpretation of the coefficients, it should be noted that both, τ and v_1, are expressed in percentage terms. The other three volatility measures, v_2, v_3 and v_4, are not as easily transformed, and thus remain as calculated.

The first specification without terms in τ and v is included as a benchmark case. For each of the five specifications including τ and v, four separate regressions were run: one for each of the four measures of volatility (as described above). However, Tables 6.4 and 6.5 initially only report for each specification the results for the regressions using v_1. Only where the use of a different measure of volatility led to significantly different results (either in terms of the coefficients, or their significance) is more than one set of results reported. Overall, it can be said that the results are fairly insensitive to the choice of volatility measure.

In terms of the regression diagnostics, both sets of regressions (for the NBTT and ITT) exhibit considerable degrees of heteroskedasticity. For this reason all the estimates presented in the tables are 'robust' OLS estimates. These heteroskedasticity-consistent estimates are based on White (1980). The reasons for the presence of heteroskedasticity are not entirely clear. One conjecture might be that the standard capital and labour growth proxies used in our regressions are not entirely appropriate. It is well known that their use requires the not particularly plausible assumptions of constant capital–output and labour force–output ratios, and a constant labour force participation rate. Moreover, the relationship between output and these two proxies is assumed to hold across the entire sample in all our specifications. From an inference point of view this is a justifiable assumption, since the aim of this paper is to analyse the effects of the terms of trade variables on output growth. However, there is a whole range of other possible specifications that also allow the relationship between output, capital and labour to vary between countries, which could be subject to further investigation.

The full sample estimates also presented a high degree of nonnormality, which led us to undertake an outlier search in the residuals and elimination from the sample of those series where the residuals were greater than 2 standard errors. The second to bottom row in both Table 6.2 and 6.3 provides a list with those countries excluded. Ideally, one should only exclude observations if a convincing argument can be made that these countries have been significantly affected by exogenous factors. Certainly, Botswana, Kuwait and Yemen are all very small countries that have made large windfall gains though raw material price shocks during our sample period. In contrast, China, Korea, and again, Botswana, are countries where the exogenous 'input' may be particularly good economic management. More possible stories might be found, but for each 'story' there are other countries in the sample that would also qualify, but do not constitute significant outliers. Hence, our main justification for the exclusion of these outliers is the need to achieve normality in the estimated residuals. The third diagnostic test of interest is the LM test (Reset test) for omitted variables. It allows us to reject mis-specification of the regression equation in the vast majority of cases.

Looking now at Table 6.3 presenting the results for the net barter terms of trade, we first of all find that the terms of trade variables add only a modest amount of explanatory power compared with the benchmark case (Specification 1). The adjusted R^2 rises from 0.32 to between 0.35 and 0.40, depending on the specification used. In many cases, the standard error actually rises. Specification 2, for instance, which has no subgroupings, shows both, τ and v, to be insignificant. Specification 3 which divides the samples into three categories according to per-capita income levels, shows a positive terms of trade trend effect for low-income countries, but none for middle- or high-income countries. Of the volatility variables, only v_4 gives any significant result: a negative impact for high-income countries.

Specification 4 divides the sample into Sub-Saharan African (SSA) countries, Latin American countries and the remainder grouped together. In particular, this was done to examine the claim that SSA countries somehow do not perform quite like other countries. Here the four volatility measures provide very similar results, so only those with v_1 are reported. We find the expected results for the 'control' group: a significant positive effect of the terms of trade trend and a significant negative effect of terms of trade volatility. However, the results for the SSA and LA subgroups are not of the expected nature. The Latin American countries seem to have benefited from volatility, and be negatively affected by positive trend changes. For the SSA subgroup, one obtains a mildly significant, though overall positive, effect of volatility on growth. Specification 4 is the only one where the intercept variables are significant. The negative coefficients for both the SSA and LA intercept dummies, indicate the presence of significant exogenous factors negatively affecting these countries' growth rate[11].

The fifth and sixth specifications divide the countries according

Table 6.4 Net barter terms of trade (dependent variable: y; method of estimation: OLS (Robust))

v used	1	2	3a	3b	v used:	4	v used:	5a	5b	v used:	6
	-	vl	vl	v4		vl		vl	v3		vl
constant	-0.530 (-0.95)	-0.434 (-0.53)	-0.503 (-0.44)	-0.142 (-0.13)	constant	2.668 (2.87)	constant	0.287 (0.22)	0.007 (0.01)	constant	0.549 (0.58)
- low inc.			0.712 (0.69)	-0.154 (-0.13)	- S.S.A.	-4.037 (-3.33)	- oil exp.	-2.172 (-1.29)	-0.141 (-0.17)	- LDC oil exp.	-2.069 (-1.04)
- high inc.			1.095 (0.79)	1.635 (1.08)	- L.A.	-5.006 (-4.27)	- man exp.	0.309 (0.26)	0.988 (1.15)	- LDC man exp.	2.726 (1.02)
										- LDC pr. exp.	-0.480 (-0.38)
I/Y	15.124 (6.64)	14.721 (6.24)	12.503 (4.98)	12.170 (5.20)	I/Y	7.502 (3.10)	I/Y	11.632 (4.41)	11.870 (4.51)	I/Y	12.116 (4.22)
gpop	0.539 (4.44)	0.501 (3.82)	0.553 (2.55)	0.577 (2.70)	gpop	1.049 (6.18)	gpop	0.601 (3.07)	0.635 (3.14)	gpop	0.557 (2.20)
trend		0.033 (0.37)	-0.135 (-1.20)	-0.089 (-0.91)	trend	0.251 (2.12)	trend	0.108 (0.71)	0.108 (0.71)	trend	0.483 (1.39)
- low inc.			0.467 (3.00)	0.390 (2.87)	- S.S.A.	-0.146 (-0.74)	- oil exp.	-0.936 (-3.55)	-0.931 (-3.59)	- LDC oil exp.	-1.290 (-3.05)
- high inc.			0.030 (0.13)	0.064 (0.30)	- L.A.	-0.434 (-2.12)	- man exp.	0.561 (2.35)	0.571 (2.40)	- LDC man exp.	-0.265 (-0.56)
										- LDC pr. exp.	-0.354 (-0.97)
volatility		0.009 (0.38)	0.028 (0.86)	0.066 (0.26)	volatility	-0.088 (-2.32)	volatility	-0.021 (-0.43)	-152.8 (-0.48)	volatility	0.060 (1.13)
- low inc.			-0.036 (-0.77)	0.046 (0.12)	- S.S.A.	0.108 (1.94)	- oil exp.	0.153 (1.97)	475.2 (1.38)	- LDC oil exp.	0.061 (0.73)
- high inc.			-0.116 (-1.67)	-1.225 (-1.96)	- L.A.	0.185 (3.17)	- man exp.	0.112 (1.37)	1113.3 (2.03)	- LDC man exp.	-0.235 (-0.86)
										- LDC pr. exp.	-0.067 (-0.88)
s.e.	1.489	1.501	1.434	1.425	s.e.	1.483	s.e.	1.596	1.602	s.e.	1.625
R^2	0.334	0.339	0.411	0.419	R^2	0.460	R^2	0.423	0.419	R^2	0.450
R^2 (adj)	0.319	0.308	0.339	0.348	R^2 (adj)	0.396	R^2 (adj)	0.355	0.350	R^2 (adj)	0.361
Heterosk	9.521**	15.781**	39.943**	38.534***	Heterosk	31.107**	Heterosk	47.982**	47.411**	Heterosk	72.106**
Normality	0.707	0.759	0.059	0.186	Normality	1.762	Normality	0.031	0.065	Normality	0.364
Reset:	2.169	3.780	5.846	4.334	Reset:	2.545	Reset:	5.045	2.542	Reset:	8.948*
Omitted countries:	Botswana, Guyana, Korea, Kuwait, Niger, Yemen, Zambia	Botswana, Guyana, Korea, Kuwait, Niger, Yemen,	Botswana, China, Hong Kong, Korea, Niger, Yemen	Botswana, Jamaica, Niger,	Omitted countries:	Botswana, Jamaica, Kuwait, Yemen	Omitted countries:	Botswana, Indonesia, Korea, Niger	Botswana, Indonesia, Jamaica, Niger	Omitted countries:	Botswana, Indonesia, Jamaica, Niger
n	92	92	93	93	n	95	n	95	95	n	95

Notes:
'Robust' OLS estimates heteroskedasticity-consistent standard errors. The numbers in brackets are t-ratios. The heteroskedasticity test is a White LM test and refers to the normal OLS (non-robust) estimate. The test for normality is a Jarque-Bera test. The Reset test is a LM test for omitted variables. n is the sample size for each estimated equation. The omitted countries were selected on the basis of an outlier search in the residuals. An asterisk * marks a null hypothesis rejection at a 5% significance level, two ** at a 1% significance level.

Table 6.5 Income terms of trade (dependent variable: y; method of estimation: OLS (Robust))

				Regression no.				
	1	2	3a	3b			4a	4b
v used	-	v1	v1	v3	v used:		v1	v3
constant	-0.473 (-0.82)	0.098 (0.20)	0.212 (0.30)	0.154 (0.24)	**constant**		0.600 (0.98)	0.308 (0.49)
– low inc.			-0.171 (-0.31)	0.194 (0.50)	– S.S.A.		-1.219 (-2.09)	-0.501 (-0.88)
– high inc.			-0.152 (-0.18)	-1.246 (-1.80)	– L.A.		-0.213 (-0.37)	-0.285 (-0.55)
I/Y	14.557 (6.14)	6.946 (3.74)	6.470 (3.35)	5.596 (2.98)	I/Y		3.785 (2.04)	3.847 (2.05)
gpop	0.569 (4.51)	0.640 (4.99)	0.599 (3.94)	0.608 (4.07)	**gpop**		0.891 (6.37)	0.877 (6.79)
trend		0.292 (8.33)	0.363 (7.51)	0.370 (7.83)	**trend**		0.340 (3.82)	0.373 (4.42)
– low inc.			-0.116 (-1.53)	-0.119 (-1.55)	– S.S.A.		-0.165 (-1.60)	-0.193 (-1.96)
– high inc.			0.272 (1.63)	0.245 (1.96)	– L.A.		-0.041 (-0.40)	-0.061 (-0.63)
volatility		-0.006 (-0.68)	-0.016 (-1.38)	-45.82 (-1.93)	**volatility**		-0.023 (-1.03)	-137.9 (-2.04)
– low inc.			0.027 (1.67)	62.95 (2.15)	– S.S.A.		0.048 (1.97)	170.6 (2.50)
– high inc.			-0.200 (-5.65)	-615.24 (-8.76)	– L.A.		0.000 (0.02)	98.1 (1.40)
s.e.	1.495	1.174	1.119	1.073	s.e.		1.110	1.100
R^2	0.300	0.629	0.690	0.715	R^2		0.681	0.687
R^2 (adj)	0.284	0.612	0.651	0.679	R^2 (adj)		0.641	0.648
Heterosk	9.273**	18.768**	38.813**	42.386***	Heterosk		51.109**	36.981**
Normality	0.947	3.401	0.536	0.406	Normality		1.348	1.305
Reset:	3.133	8.401*	2.630	5.359	Reset:		7.392	6.833
Omitted countries:	Botswana, Guyana, Korea, Kuwait, Niger, Yemen, Zambia	Botswana, Burundi, Kuwait, Niger, Yemen	Botswana, Burundi, Jordan, Malta, Niger, Yemen	Botswana, Burundi, Jordan, Malta, Niger, Yemen	Omitted countries:		Botswana, Kuwait, Malta, Niger, Yemen	
n	89	91	90	90	n		91	91

Table 6.5 Income terms of trade (dependent variable: y; method of estimation: OLS (Robust)) (continued)

v used:	5a v1		5b v2		v used:	6a v1		6b v3	
constant	0.540	(0.92)	0.613	(1.06)	**constant**	-0.093	(-0.15)	0.182	(0.30)
– oil exp.	1.076	(1.51)	0.862	(1.25)	– LDC oil. exp.	2.439	(2.01)	1.221	(1.09)
– man exp.	-1.181	(-2.44)	-1.286	(-2.67)	– LDC man exp.	0.777	(0.62)	0.726	(0.94)
					– LDC pr. pr. exp.	1.120	(1.36)	0.455	(0.62)
I/Y	5.926	(2.92)	5.893	(2.87)	**I/Y**	5.768	(2.75)	5.798	(2.71)
gpop	0.666	(4.60)	0.654	(4.50)	**gpop**	0.490	(2.39)	0.559	(2.76)
trend	0.261	(8.35)	0.265	(9.04)	**trend**	0.284	(2.97)	0.279	(3.09)
– oil exp.	-0.071	(-0.77)	-0.071	(-0.76)	– LDC oil. exp.	-0.097	(-0.73)	-0.079	(-0.57)
– man exp.	0.067	(0.87)	0.045	(0.74)	– LDC man exp.	0.004	(0.03)	0.051	(0.35)
					– LDC pr. pr. exp.	-0.014	(-0.13)	-0.004	(-0.04)
volatility	-0.028	(-1.93)	-17.36	(-2.29)	**volatility**	0.053	(1.64)	359.7	(1.48)
– oil exp.	0.004	(0.18)	8.30	(0.85)	– LDC oil. exp.	-0.081	(-2.14)	-390.1	(-1.58)
– man exp.	0.107	(2.72)	66.86	(3.10)	– LDC man exp.	0.044	(-0.51)	-595.3	(-1.47)
					– LDC pr. pr. exp.	-0.073	(-2.06)	-461.9	(-1.86)
s.e.	1.128		1.114		s.e.	1.249		1.247	
R^2	0.681		0.689		R^2	0.622		0.623	
R^2 (adj)	0.642		0.650		R^2 (adj)	0.559		0.560	
Heterosk	35.897**		35.632**		Heterosk	41.893**		43.426**	
Normality	1.688		1.269		Normality	2.864		3.957	
Reset:	5.790		4.584		Reset:	11.364**		10.758**	
Omitted countries:	Botswana, Burundi, Kuwait, Niger, Yemen		Botswana, Kuwait, Niger, Yemen		Omitted countries:	Botswana, Kuwait, Niger, Yemen			
n	91		91		n	92		92	

Note: See Table 6.4.

114

to export structure, the former grouping all counties, and the latter separating out the developing countries. Three sets of terms of trade coefficients are significant. In all regressions the oil-exporters exhibit a negative effect from the trend term. It seems, therefore, that these countries have obtained their favourable terms of trade at the expense of restrictions in output.

The manufacturing exporters (all countries) show the expected positive terms of trade trend effect. With respect to volatility, the significant coefficients are again positive. In 5a, the coefficient on volatility for the oil exporters is mildly significant. In 5b, it is the manufacturing exporters who seem to respond positively to volatility effects. Overall, Specification 6 is probably the least 'successful', in that most of the added interactive dummies are insignificant. It is also the only one of the six specifications where the Reset test indicates the possible omission of relevant explanatory variables.

To summarize thus the results for the NBTT, we are left with a mixed bag of evidence on the effects of net barter terms of trade trend and volatility. We get both positive (for low-income countries) and negative (Latin American countries and oil-exporters) effects from the trend component in the terms of trade. The same is true for volatility, where we also find several, somewhat unexpected, positive (SSA, LA, oil- and manufacturing-exporting countries) effects, as well as two negative effects (high-income countries, and the 'other countries' group in 4) on growth. However, when taking the sample as a whole, the two variables are insignificant.

Do the income terms of trade provide us with a different picture? The same specifications were estimated, and the results are presented in Table 6.4. The first observation is that the inclusion of the income terms of trade variables approximately doubles the R^2 statistics, and substantially lowers the regression standard errors compared to Specification 1, our benchmark case. The overall trend variable is positive and highly significant in all specifications. The only exception to this can be found in regression 4a, where the interactive dummy for the SSA countries has a negative, marginally significant, coefficient, although the total trend effect for the SSA countries remains positive ($\gamma_3 + \gamma_4 = 0.373 - 0.193 = 0.180$). The interactive trend dummies in Specifications 5 and 6, where countries are divided according to export structures, are all insignificant, furthering the evidence in favour of a universally positive effect of the ITT trend on output growth.

As with the NBTT, the volatility effects in the ITT regressions provide a rather mixed picture. The overall volatility effect, in Specification 2, is statistically insignificant[12]. There is strong evidence, however, for negative effects of volatility on growth in regressions 3a and 3b. The coefficient for the middle-income countries in 3a is also mildly significant, with a t-ratio of −1.93 (p-value: 0.057). In regression 4b, too, the non-African or Latin American countries' growth rate shows a negative correlation with terms of trade volatility. For low income countries, the picture is reversed: In 3b, the positive (and significant) coefficient on volatility outweighs that of the control group, and in the Specification 4 regressions the SSA countries also appear to benefit from greater volatility. In Specifications 5 and 6 we find that it is the primary product exporters (5a, 5b, and for LDCs in 6b), and the LDC oil-exporters (6a) that seem to be significantly, negatively affected by ITT volatility. The overall group of manufacturing exporters, both LDCs and industrialized countries, on the other hand exhibit a positive relationship between output growth and ITT volatility (5a and 5b).

The diagnostics for the ITT regressions are fairly similar to those reported earlier for the NBTT. All regressions had to be estimated by 'robust' OLS due to a significant degree of heteroskedasticity. Normality could again only be achieved via the exclusion of significant outliers. Details are provided in Table 6.4. The Reset test for omitted variables again shows Specification 6 to be least 'successful' – the LM test rejects the null hypothesis of no omission of significant explanatory variables at a low significance level (p-values of the LM test for the four different regressions for Specification 6 range from 0.008 to 0.013). In the case of the ITT, Specification 4 also comes close to rejecting the Reset test (p-values between 0.046 and 0.077).

A last issue concerns the relevant lines along which the countries in the sample should be divided. We find strong evidence that volatility and trend in the terms of trade do not affect output growth homogeneously across countries. This is not only true for the size and significance of the coefficients, but also their sign. Hence any conclusions derived from this type of analysis must be interpreted in this light.

To summarize the findings of this section, we have found the following:

1. The initial analysis of the trend and volatility components in the terms of trade showed that the oil-exporting countries experienced by far the greatest levels of volatility over the 1968–88 period. With respect to the trend in the terms of trade, the NBTT and the ITT provided contrasting pictures. Whereas the oil-exporters saw the only overall positive trend in the NBTT, they were not necessarily the countries with the largest ITT trends. This, and the comparatively poor showing of the group of Sub-Saharan countries with respect to the ITT trend, supports the view that the volume of exports is a very important factor in determining the ability to import.

2. The econometric analysis of the effects of volatility and trends in the terms of trade resulted in a mixed picture. In general, the explanatory power of these variables in the case of the NBTT was considerably less than for the ITT. This is not surprising, as it is the ability to import which drives many of the theoretical arguments of why the terms of trade may affect output growth. The trend terms are mostly positive, where significant, although their effect on growth appears to be insignificant for the NBTT when the sample is considered as a whole. The estimates provided particularly strong evidence for the positive effects of the ITT trend on output growth.

3. The novel aspect of this analysis was the inclusion of a volatility variable. Four measures of volatility were used, and on the whole, the results of the various specifications estimated proved fairly insensitive to which of the four was being used. The evidence on the effects of volatility on growth is less clear. Over the sample as a whole (Specification 2), the coefficients are insignificant for both, NBTT and ITT. There is some evidence that high-income countries have been adversely affected by NBTT volatility. There is, however, also some evidence for positive effects of volatility on growth for a number of subgroups (Sub-Saharan Africa, Latin America, oil- and manufacturing exporters).

The effects of volatility in the ITT show a similar pattern. Again it is the high-income countries that appear to be negatively affected. Low-income, and especially Sub-Saharan African, countries, on the other hand, show the opposite effect, as does the group of manufacturing exporters. When splitting the developing countries into subgroups, negative volatility effects reappear for oil- and primary-product exporters. Lastly, the analysis has shown that it makes good sense to allow parameters to vary between country groups. Unfortunately, this also means that our conclusions are of a more complex nature than they might otherwise be.

The main avenue for future research into the effects of terms of trade volatility must lie in a closer examination of the time-series properties of the terms of trade variables. Clearly, the deterministic trend model used in this paper might be justified in the context of shorter sample periods like the one used in this paper, but must be examined very carefully against the possibility of stochastic trends when longer samples are available.

6.4   CONCLUSIONS

The empirical research in this paper only partly supports our conjecture that volatility in the terms of trade should have a significantly negative effect on growth. The latter is supported by the panel estimates in Section 6.2, but not by some of the cross-section results in Section 6.3. The discrepancy between these results is to some part due to the different measures of volatility employed. A second reason must be the differences in chosen methodologies. The cross-section analysis employs an augmented production function, whereas the panel estimates do not control for growth in the factors of production.

The results from the cross-section study provided a mixed picture with respect to the volatility effects. Over the entire sample, the relationship between volatility and growth is insignificant. This is true for both net barter and income terms of trade. Splitting the overall sample into subgroups changes that picture. High-income countries appear to be the ones most negatively affected by volatility. A positive relationship between volatility and growth, on the other hand, was found for several other subgroups, including Sub-Saharan and low-income countries.

It is perhaps surprising that, while volatility seems to be higher in poorer countries, its impact on GNP growth is stronger in middle- and high-income countries. This may be because in the low-income countries compensatory factors such as aid are more important and also because the income terms of trade are more related to the capacity to service debt than capacity to import. This interpretation, however, is one of several open questions – alongside the important issue of the correct representation of the trend and volatility components in the terms of trade – which must be a matter of future research.

NOTES

1. The estimated equation was:

$$Y_{it} = \text{constant} + 0.007\ TT_{it} + 0.035\ TT_{it-1} - 0.008\ TT_{it-2} -$$
$$(0.59) \qquad (3.20) \qquad (-0.71)$$

$$1.081\ VAR_{it} + 0.186\ VAR_{it-1} - 0.099\ VAR_{it-2} + 0.025\ Y_{it-1}$$
$$(-3.29) \qquad (1.12) \qquad (-0.59) \qquad (0.86)$$

adj. $R^2 = 0.113$ $n = 1264$ ($i = 1, ..., 79; t = 1, ..., 16$)
sample period: 1973–88

where Y = annual percentage change in real GNP, TT = annual percentage change in the net barter terms of trade, and VAR = volatility (measured as the log of the absolute change in the terms of trade). The regression included country and year dummies. The numbers in brackets are t-ratios.
2. The data is taken from the World Bank World Tables, for the period 1968–88. The countries in the sample (99 for the NBTT, and 96 for the ITT) were chosen purely on the basis of data availability. The countries are: Algeria, Argentina, Australia, Austria, Benin, Bolivia, Botswana, Brazil, Burkina Faso, Burundi, Cameroon, Canada, CAR, Chile, China, Colombia, Congo (PR), Costa Rica, Cote d'Ivoire, Denmark, Dominican Republic, Ecuador, Egypt, El Salvador, Ethiopia, Fiji, Finland, France, Gabon, The Gambia, Germany (FR), Ghana, Greece, Guatemala, Guyana, Haiti, Honduras, Hong Kong, Iceland, India, Indonesia, Ireland, Israel, Italy, Jamaica, Japan, Jordan, Kenya, Korea (Rep.), Kuwait, Liberia, Madagascar, Malawi, Malaysia, Mali, Malta, Mauritania, Mauritius, Mexico, Morocco, Netherlands, New Zealand, Nicaragua, Niger, Nigeria, Norway, Pakistan, Panama, Papua New Guinea, Paraguay, Peru, Philippines, Portugal, Rwanda, Senegal, Sierra Leone, Singapore, Somalia, South Africa, Spain, Sri Lanka, Sudan, Sweden, Switzerland, Syria (AR), Tanzania, Thailand, Togo, Trinidad and Tobago, Tunisia, Turkey, UK, USA, Uruguay, Yemen (AR), Yugoslavia, Zaire, Zambia, Zimbabwe.
3 For those countries where the t-ratio on β_1 falls within the interval [–1.5, +1.5], the trend τ is set equal to zero in the subsequent econometric analysis.
4. Globally, of course, the average terms of trade trend should be zero, as one country's improvement cancels out with another's deterioration. Taking account of the standard error, we cannot reject the hypothesis that the average trend is equal to zero. Ignoring the standard error, there are three possible factors making the average non-zero. First of all, our sample could be biased

Second, the terms of trade measure includes transport costs. Third, this measure, in order to represent the global average, would need to include weights based on a country's share in world trade.
5. Using an F-Test for the equality of two variances.
6. For a more appropriate measure of the capacity to import, the income terms of trade should be divided by population size. This, however, would require the calculation of an additional index based on the original export price, import price and export volume series.
7. The t-statistic is:

$$\frac{(\bar{x}_1 - \bar{x}_2)}{\sqrt{(\hat{s}_1^2 (n_1 - 1) + \hat{s}_2^2 (n_2 - 1))}} \sqrt{\frac{(n_1 n_2 (n_1 + n_2 - 2))}{(n_1 + n_2)}}$$

8. This was arbitrarily chosen for convenience, and has the advantage that the likelihood of missing a significant outlier is smaller than using the common 5 per cent significance level.
9. The first two of measures of volatility/instability, v_2 and v_3 were previously used by Gyimah-Brempong (1991), and the last, v_4 by Glezakos (1973).
10. The use and suitability of these two variables will be discussed elsewhere in this section.
11. These could be debt pressures.
12. Hence the effect of volatility across the whole sample is insignificant for both ITT and NBTT. This result is different from the significant (negative) overall effect found by Edström and Singer (1992) using panel data. The reason is likely to lie in the fact that the latter study uses the absolute value of the deviations in the terms of trade as their measure of volatility which, however, includes a trend component.

REFERENCES

Basu, P. and D. McLeod (1991): 'Terms of trade fluctuations and economic growth in developing countries', *Journal of Development Economics*, **37** (1/2), 89–110.

Campbell, J. and P. Perron (1991): 'Pitfalls and opportunities: what macroeconomists should know about unit roots', in O. Blanchard and S. Fischer (eds), *NBER Macroeconomics Annual*.

DeJong, D., J. Nankervis, N. Savin and C. Whiteman (1992): The power problems of unit root tests in time series with autoregressive errors', *Journal of Econometrics*, **53**, 323–43.

Edström, J. and H.W. Singer (1992): 'The influence of trends in barter terms of trade and of their volatility on GNP growth', Discussion Paper 312, Institute of Development Studies, University of Sussex.

Glezakos, E. (1973): 'Export instability and economic growth: a statistical verification', *Economic Development and Cultural Change*, **21** (4), 670–78.

Gyimah-Brempong, K. (1991): 'Export instability and economic growth in Sub-Saharan Africa', *Economic Development and Cultural Change*, **39** (4), 815–28.

Hart, A.G., N. Kaldor and J. Tinbergen (1964): 'The case for an international commodity reserve currency', UNCTAD.

Maizels, Alfred (1992): *Commodities in Crisis* (Oxford: Clarendon Press), 61–85.

Prebisch, R. (1950): *The Economic Development of Latin America and its Principal Problems* (New York, United Nations).

Sapsford, D., P. Sarker and H.W. Singer (1992): 'The Prebisch-Singer terms of trade hypothesis revisited', *Journal of International Development*, **4** (2), 315–32.

Sarker, P. and H.W. Singer (1991): 'Manufactured exports of developing countries and their terms of trade since 1965', *World Development*, **19** (4), 333–40.

Singer H.W. (1950): 'The distribution of gains between investing and borrowing countries', *American Economic Review*, **40**, (May), 473–85.

White, H. (1980): 'A heteroskedasticity-consistent covariance matrix and a direct test for heteroskedasticity', *Econometrica*, **48**, 817–38.

7. Does Economic Policy Influence the Price Volatility of Commodities?: An Econometric Investigation of the Rice Market in Taiwan

John-ren Chen*

7.1 INTRODUCTION

Rice is the most important staple food product and source of agricultural income in Taiwan. About 50 per cent of the crop area in Taiwan has been used for the production of rice in the last four decades. In the 1950s and 1980s respectively 150 kg and 100 kg of rice per capita was consumed. The favourable climate conditions in Taiwan enable two to three rice harvests annually. Among the agricultural products rice is still the most profitable for the farmers in Taiwan as the irrigation system for rice production and the input of pesticide (insecticide) make the yield relatively stable in comparison to other agricultural products.

As a result of its importance for the Taiwanese economy a lot of policy measures have been carried out in order to influence the price and production of rice since the 1950s. The Food Bureau of Taiwan,

* Paper presented at the Commodity Markets Conference jointly organized by CREDIT (Nottingham University) and the Department of Economics (Lancaster University) 24-26th May 1993 in Ambleside.
I am very much indebted to Gerhard Biasi for his assistance in the calculation of the regression equations. I owe much to Richard Hule for the avoidance of many errors in the mathematical derivations, and last but not least to Herbert Stocker for valuable discussion. I don't need to mention that I am solely responsible for the remaining errors.

the office responsible for rice policy, has collected rice and kept huge inventories in order to secure a sufficient supply of rice and avoid a rapid expansion of its price. Not only economic measures but also other measures, such as the time limiting of private inventories, have been introduced to avoid a rapid price increase.

Economic policy does not appear to be neutral with respect to the price volatility of commodities (Chen, 1993a) and the main purpose of this paper is to study the effects of this phenomenon. Before this is done one last point has to be mentioned. The rice market in Taiwan is a closed market since private foreign trade of rice is not permitted.

This paper is organized as follows: the background of the Taiwanese rice sector and the organization of the agricultural sector in Taiwan as well as a survey of the policy measures for the rice sector are presented in Section 7.2. In Section 7.3 four models for the rice market in Taiwan representing four periods with different policy measures are discussed along with their parameters that are estimated in structural form. The price volatility of rice is then also introduced into the discussion. In Section 7.4 the structural form of the models is studied whereby an estimation of the structural equations and the reduced equation for the price of rice is made. Here, we hope to substantiate the propositions studied in the above sections with a comparison of the estimated parameters of the models in structural form with the reduced equation for the price of rice.

In Appendix A a microeconomic foundation for the behaviour of rice producers in Taiwan is introduced subject to differing policy measures for the rice sector. The four important and different policy measures imposed by the Taiwanese authorities make the construction of four different microeconomic production models for rice necessary. In Appendix B the microeconomic foundation for consumer behaviour is discussed.

7.2 THE BACKGROUND AND THE IMPORTANT POLICY MEASURES OF THE RICE SECTOR IN TAIWAN

The Background of Rice Production in Taiwan

Taiwanese agriculture is characterized by a number of small family

farm units most of which are land-owning farmers and rice-produ-
cers. Only about 15 and 5 per cent of them were tenant farmers in
the 1950s and 1980s respectively. The average area of cultivated
land per farm has amounted to about 1.1 ha on average in the last
four decades and the rent has been set at 37.5 per cent of the main
produce since the land reform. As a result most farm units regularly use their own land and family labour forces. The irrigation
that is necessary for rice production is supplied by a public irrigation system that has been steadily improved since the Japanese
colonial age. The irrigation fees are paid according to the amount
of land input used in the rice production. The only variable input
that has to be bought by the farmers is chemical fertilizer, which is
supplied by the Food Bureau. The fertilizer price is set by the
government. In the 1950s and 1960s the fertilizer price for rice
production was set at more than twice that of the world market
price in order to secure a source of tax revenue for the government.
In the last two decades, however, the fertilizer price has been
reduced considerably.

During the last two decades of rapid economic development in
Taiwan the share of the agricultural labour force has fallen from
about 60 per cent at the beginning of the 1950s to around 15 per cent
of the total labour force last year. The input of capital is therefore
necessary to maintain the prevailing level of agricultural production.
Due to the small scale of farms in Taiwan a profitable investment
from their side cannot be expected. To enable the input of capital,
associations of agricultural machinery that supply the capital
services to the farmers have been organized. The fees for the capital
services demanded by the farmers are set relative to land input.

Policy Measures since the 1950s

The fertilizer–rice exchange programme (from 1949 to 1972)

Among the policy measures for the rice sector the fertilizer–rice
exchange programme was the most important regarding the regulation of rice production and the attainment of rice by the Food
Bureau for the public sector and for public rice inventories.

The supply of fertilizer for rice production was distributed to the
rice producers directly by the local organizations of the Taiwan
Farmer Association for the Food Bureau. After the harvest the
farmers had to pay for the fertilizer in rice, which was also

collected by the local organization of the Taiwan Farmer Association for the Food Bureau. The price of fertilizer was set in units of rice. The exchange rate for 1 kg of ammonium sulphate, calcium ammonium nitrate, and calcium superphosphate was 1 kg, 1 kg and 0.4 kg rice in 1951 and reduced gradually to 0.53, 0.49, and 0.37 kg in 1972 respectively.

In an earlier study the author found that the increasing input of fertilizer was the one important factor most responsible for the increasing productivity in the production of rice from 1952 to 1969. The share of the cost of fertilizer input relative to the yield of rice amounted to about 28 per cent on average in the same period. This means that the Food Bureau acquired about 28 per cent of the rice production from this source in the same period (Chen, 1975).

The fertilizer–rice exchange programme was stopped in 1972 and the Food Bureau has supplied fertilizer for the rice farmers since then. Instead of the fertilizer–rice exchange rate the price of fertilizer has been set in units of the New Taiwan dollar and the farmer has had the choice of paying for the fertilizer either in rice or in currency. The fertilizer price set by the Food Bureau is announced before the production season.

The land tax payment in rice
To collect rice required for government usage the land tax has been paid in kind (rice) since 1946. The land tax is given in units of so called 'Land Tax Dollars' for crop land. Since then the government has announced the exchange rate of the Land Tax Dollar to rice which rose from 8.85 kg rice per Land Tax Dollar in 1946 to 26.35 kg in 1967. The farmers have to pay the land tax in rice after the harvest.

Before the implementation of the fertilizer–rice exchange programme this measure was the main contributor to the government holding of rice.

Compulsive sale of rice by the farmers linked to the land tax payment in rice
To collect more rice for government needs the rice farmers had to sell rice to the Food Bureau in proportion to the land tax at a price set by the government. This was lower than the market price before 1972. Since then the price has been guaranteed at a level not lower than the support price which was introduced in 1974.

Support price for the rice farmers
The support price measure for rice was introduced in 1974. A special Food Stabilization Fund totalling 3 billion New Taiwan Dollars was established in order to buy rice from the rice farmers at the support price. From 1974 to 1976 there was no limit on the amount of rice that the farmers could sell to the Food Bureau at the support price. In this period the price support measure caused a huge production surplus of rice in Taiwan. Due to this a sale limit (970 kg per ha) for the rice farmers has been implemented since 1977 and the support price is announced shortly before the planting season.

Since 1974/75 as the fertilizer–rice exchange programme was given up the price support programme has been the Food Bureau's main source for the obtainment of rice for government requirements and the public inventory. In 1974/75 (from 1 July 1974 to 30 June 1975) about 39 per cent of the rice obtained by the Food Bureau was contributed by the price support programme. This share reached a record of 87.5 per cent in 1983/84 (from 1 July 1983 to 30 June 1984) and has been sustained at more than 80 per cent since 1981/82.

The rice holding of the Taiwan Food Bureau
The Taiwan Food Bureau has kept a huge rice inventory in order to secure the supply for government needs and stabilize the price of rice. The government requires rice for military consumption, for public workers' salaries, which are paid in rice, and the special needs of public schools and public short term schools, etc. To prevent short-term price increases the Food Bureau often supplies rice from its inventory. The Food Bureau's rice inventory may be compared to the buffer stock measure discussed in commodity stabilization policy.

The time limit for private inventories during times of rapid price increases
This measure was frequently used in the Fifties and Sixties. At times of rapid price increases in rice it was not permitted to keep a private inventory for longer than ten days after the date of obtaining the inventory. This measure would have been very effective if it had been fully enforced.

The export and import of rice
There is no free trade of rice in Taiwan. The export and import of rice in Taiwan are carried out by the Food Bureau according to the directives of the central government. Thus the export and import of rice can be regarded as exogenous. Taiwan is normally a net exporter of rice and only imports rice in order to fill short-term gaps in domestic supply.

7.3 THE MODELS FOR THE RICE MARKET IN TAIWAN

Due to the underlying microeconomic behavioural relationships under consideration of the different policy measures carried out in this period we need four models for the rice market in Taiwan since the 1950s (Chen, 1993b). We have constructed a model for the period from 1952 to 1972 in which the fertilizer rice exchange programme was implemented, a model for 1973 with the main characteristic of a free market, a model from 1974 to 1976 with a support price programme and a model for the period since 1977 with a partial support price programme. As we discuss in Appendix A the underlying microeconomic behavioural relationship for the rice farmers differs in these four different models although the microeconomic demand behavioural relationship may be the same for all four models.

In an earlier paper (Chen, 1975) a regression equation for the per capita annual consumption of rice in Taiwan was estimated from 1953 to 1969. In this regression equation the per capita annual consumption of rice in Taiwan showed a highly significant positive dependence on the price of rice and a 'negative' one on per capita income. This surprising result is explained in another paper (Chen, 1993c). A theoretical reason for this behaviour is given in the Appendix B.

For simplicity we will specify these models with linear functions. Additionally, a double logarithmic function could be used as an alternative functional form.

The Model from the 1950s to 1972

As a result of the fact that the producers of rice in Taiwan have to pay the land tax and for fertilizer in rice while the sale of rice is linked to the land tax paid to the Food Bureau, only a part of the rice yield is sold on the market. Therefore, the supply of rice on the market is the surplus of rice yield reduced by the amount collected by the Food Bureau. The Food Bureau used three measures to obtain rice in this period, namely the fertilizer–rice exchange programme, the payment of land tax in rice and the sale of rice to the Food Bureau linked to the land tax. Since the amount of rice collected by the Food Bureau (T) from the last two measures is proportional to the size of arable land the total amount of rice taken off the market is equal to:

$$T_t = w'_{1t} x^*_{1t} + \beta_t x_{3t}$$

where w'_{1t}: the fertilizer rice exchange rate;
$\quad\quad x^*_{1t}$: fertilizer input;
$\quad\quad \beta_t$: the sum of the land tax rate and the sale rate
$\quad\quad\quad$ proportional to the land tax rate;
$\quad\quad x_{3t}$: land input;
$\quad\quad t$: year.

According to the results of microeconomic behaviour shown in another paper (see Appendix A and Chen, 1993b) the amount of rice paid for the input of fertilizer can be specified as:

$$w'_{1t} x^*_{1t} = \alpha \bar{Q}^*_t, \text{ where } \alpha \text{ is the share of expected yield } (\bar{Q}^*_t)$$
$$\text{paid for the fertilizer input } (x^*_{1t})$$
$$\alpha \text{ is a constant in the case of a Cobb-Douglas}$$
$$\text{production function.}$$

The market supply of rice in the period t (S_t) can now be defined as the difference between rice production and the amount of rice collected by the Food Bureau:

$$S_t = Q^*_t - w'_{1t} x^*_{1t} - \beta_t x_{3t} = (1 - \alpha)\,\bar{Q}^*_t - \beta_t x_{3t} + u_t$$
$$\text{where } Q^*_t = \bar{Q}^*_t + u_t \text{ a random variable}$$

We assume a linear supply function for the farmers as a linear approximation of the microeconomic behaviour derived above:

$$Q^*_t = b'_0 - b'_1 w'_{1t} + b'_2 x_{2t} + b'_3 x_{3t} + b'_4 t + u_t$$
$$\text{where } x_{2t}: \text{labour input, } t: \text{trend for technical progress}$$
$$b'_i > 0 \text{ for } i = 1, 2, 3, 4.$$

The resulting market supply function is then specified as follows:

$$S_t = b_0 - b_1 w'_{1t} + b_2 x_{2t} + b_3 x_{3t} + b_4 t + u_t$$

where $b_i = (1 - \alpha) b'_i$ for $i = 0, 2, 4$ and

$$b_3 = (1 - \alpha) b'_3 - \beta_t > 0$$

The market demand (D) is defined as the difference between total consumption (C) and the consumption related to the requirements of the Food Bureau (G), i.e. the armed forces' rice consumption, the public workers' salary, which is paid in rice, and the rice provided for social programmes:

$$D_t = C_t - G_t$$

Total consumption is equal to the product of the population (B) and per capita consumption. Due to the per capita consumption function derived in Chen (1993c) we now specify a linear function as its linear approximation:

$$C_t = a_0 + a_1 P_t - a_2 Y_t - a_3 P_{jt} + a_4 C_{t-1} + (1 - a_5) G_t + v_t$$

where: P_t: market price of rice
Y_t: per capita income
P_j: price of other food (pork)
G_t: consumption provided by the Food Bureau
v_t: a random variable

Alternatively we can specify the per capita consumption of rice as shown in the microeconomic behavioural relationship (Chen, 1993c) and use the identity $C_t = B_t.c_t$ where c_t is the per capita consumption of rice.

Rice can only be stored for a short time in Taiwan without a considerable reduction in its quality. Under martial law during the period from 1947 until the end of 1980s the private inventories had to be sold at times of price increases. In this period martial law was imposed effectively against the so-called speculators who had been storing rice (the main food). Therefore the share of private inventories in this period was only very small. The Food Bureau is the only institution in Taiwan that stores considerable amounts of rice. After substituting the above demand and supply functions into the equilibrium condition the reduced equation for the market price of rice is equal to:

$$P_t^* = \frac{1}{a_1}[(b_0 - a_0) + a_2 Y_t + a_3 P_{jt} - a_4 C_{t-1} - b_1 w_{1t}' + b_2 x_{2t} +$$

$$b_3 x_{3t} + b_4 t + a_5 G_t + u_t - v_t]$$

Applying the methods from Newberry and Stiglitz (1981) Y, P_j, x_2, and x_3 are systematic risks, while u and v are non-systematic risks. Assuming stochastic independence of these risks the price volatility of rice can be given as:

$$\text{Var}(P^*) = \left(\frac{1}{a_1}\right)^2 [a_2^2 \text{Var}(Y) + a_3^2 \text{Var}(P_j) +$$

$$+ b_2^2 \text{Var}(x_2) + b_3^2 \text{Var}(x_3) + \text{Var}(u) + \text{Var}(v)]$$

where $\text{Var}(x)$ denotes the variance of x

In the calculation of the above price volatility the fertilizer rice exchange rate, the land tax rate, the amount of rice to be sold to the Food Bureau relative to the land tax and the rice consumption provided by the government are politically controllable variables and therefore non-stochastic.

The price volatility of the nonsystematic risks is given as:

$$\left(\frac{1}{a_1}\right)^2 [\text{Var}(u) + \text{Var}(v)]$$

We will make an estimation for both the model in structural form and the reduced equation for the market price. The results of the estimation will be given and discussed below.

The Model for 1973

Due to the microeconomic behavioural relationships discussed in Appendix A the specification of the market supply function for 1973 can be given as:

$$S_t = Q_t^* - \beta_t x_{3t}$$

$$= b_0 + b_1 \bar{P}_t - b_2 w_{1t} + b_3 x_{2t} + (b_4 - \beta_t) x_{3t} + b_5 t + u_t$$

where $\bar{P}_t$: expected price during the planting season,

$$P_t = \bar{P}_t + v_t$$

w_{1t} : fertilizer price in units of the New Taiwan Dollar

For an explanation of all other symbols see above.

The market demand function as specified above can also be applied in the present model. The reduced equation for the market price is calculated as:

$$P_t^* = \frac{1}{a_1 - b_1} [(b_0 - a_0) + a_2 Y_t + a_3 P_{jt} - a_4 C_{t-1} + a_5 G_t - b_2 w_{1t}$$
$$+ b_3 x_{2t} + (b_4 - \beta_t) x_{3t} + b_5 t + u_t - v_t]$$

The price volatility is given as:

$$\text{Var}(P^*) = \left(\frac{1}{a_1 - b_1}\right)^2 [a_2^2 \text{ Var}(Y) + a_3^2 \text{ Var}(P_j) + b_2^2 \text{ Var}(w_1)$$
$$+ b_3^2 \text{ Var}(x_2) + b_4^2 \text{ Var}(x_3) + \text{Var}(u) + \text{Var}(v)]$$

An estimation of this model is not possible since we have a sample with only one observation.

The Model 1974–76

Analogical to the preceding sections the market supply function for 1974–76 can be specified as:

$$S_t = Q_t^* - \beta_t x_{3t}$$
$$= b_0 + b_1 g_t - b_2 w_{1t} + b_3 x_{2t} + (b_4 - \beta_t) x_{3t} + b_5 t + u_t$$

where g_t : the support price in year t

β_t : the land tax rate given in units of rice

For an explanation of all other symbols see above.

The same market demand function as the one used in the model for 1952–72 can be used in the present model. The reduced equation for the market price is calculated as:

$$P_t^* = \frac{1}{a_1} [b_0 - a_0 + a_2 Y_t + a_3 P_{jt} - a_4 C_{t-1} + a_5 G_t + b_1 g_t - b_2 w_{1t}$$
$$+ b_3 x_{2t} + (b_4 - \beta_t) x_{3t} + b_5 t + u_t - v_t]$$

The price volatility is equal to:

$$\text{Var}(P^*) = \left(\frac{1}{a_1}\right)^2 [a_2^2 \text{ Var}(Y) + a_3^2 \text{ Var}(P_j) + b_2^2 \text{ Var}(w_1) +$$
$$(b_4 - \beta_t)^2 \text{ Var}(x_3) + \text{Var}(u) + \text{Var}(v)]$$

As a result of the small amount of observations an estimation of this model can't be made.

The Model since 1977

The rice economy in Taiwan since 1974 has been characterized by a surplus of production as martial law has not been enforced effectively enough to restrict private stores of rice. The private sector has thus held a considerable share of the rice inventory in Taiwan since then. Therefore we have not only to specify the production and the consumption but also the private inventory behaviour in the present model. According to the usual specification (see, for example, Turnovsky, 1983) the private inventory function can be described by the following linear equation:

$$H_t = H_{t-1} + h(P_{t+1}^e - P_t) \quad \text{with } h > 0$$

where H_t : planned private carry-on from t to $t+1$

P_{t+1}^e : expected price made in t for $t+1$

The price expectation in the period t–1 for t is:

$$P_t^e = g_t + \pi_1(g_{t-1} - P_{t-1}), \quad 1 \geq \pi_1 \geq 0$$

This is a very simple rule used for the calculation of expectations. The expected price for the period t in $t - 1$ is equal to the support price for that period and the correction of the difference between the support price and the market price in the last period. In recent models on commodity markets rational expectation is often applied. I don't believe, however, that it is suitable for the modelling of the rice market in Taiwan.

Substituting P_{t+1}^e into the function of private inventory:

$$H_t - H_{t-1} = hg_{t+1} + h_1 g_t - h_2 P_t$$
$$\text{where } h_1 = h\pi_1 > 0, \ h_2 = h(1 + \pi_1) > 0$$

The market supply function is defined as:

$$S_t = Q_t^* - T_t^* - (H_t - H_{t-1})$$

where T_t^* is the amount of rice collected by the Food Bureau.

Applying the results of the microeconomic behavioural relationships in Chen (1993b) for Q_t^* and T_t^* (see Appendix A7.4, since 1977 the function of market supply can be given as:

$$S_t = [1 - \frac{\alpha_3}{s}(g_t - P_t) - \alpha_3 \beta_t] \, Q_t^* - h g_{t+1} - h_1(g_t - P_t)$$

where $1 > \dfrac{\alpha_3}{s}(g_t - P_t) + \alpha_3 \beta_t > 0$

α_3: output elasticity of land

$$Q_t^* = b_0' + b_1' P_t^e - b_2' w_{1t} + b_3' x_{2t} + b_4' t + u_t$$

Considering the price expectation in the above equation:

$$Q_t^* = b_0' + b_1'[g_t + \pi_1(g_{t-1} - P_{t-1})] - b_2' w_{1t} + b_3' x_{2t} + b_4' t + u_t$$

After substituting this equation into the market supply function and applying linear approximation we can specify the following linear function of the market supply:

$$S_t = b_0 + b_1 P_t + h g_{t+1} + b_2 g_t - b_3 P_{t-1} + b_4 g_{t-1} - b_5 w_{1t}$$
$$+ b_6 x_{2t} + b_7 t - b_8 \beta_t + u_t$$

The market demand function specified above can be used in the present model. Using the equilibrium condition we can derive the following reduced equation for the market price.

$$P_t^* = \frac{1}{a_1 - b_1}[b_0 - a_0 + h g_{t+1} + b_2 g_t - b_3 P_{t-1} + b_4 g_{t-1} - b_5 w_{1t} +$$
$$+ b_6 x_{2t} - b_7 t + b_8 \beta_t + a_2 Y_t + a_3 P_{jt} - a_4 C_{t-1} + a_5 G_t +$$
$$+ (u_t - v_t)]$$

Using $P_t = P_{t-1}$ the price volatility can be calculated as follows:

$$\text{Var}(P^*) = \left(\frac{1}{a_1 - b_1 + b_3}\right)^2 [a_2^2 \, \text{Var}(Y) + a_3^2 \, \text{Var}(P_j) + b_5^2 \, \text{Var}(w_1)$$
$$+ \text{Var}(u) + \text{Var}(v)]$$

Comparison of the Price Volatility

The influence of economic policy on the price volatility of rice can be shown by comparing the price volatility calculated in the four market models for rice in the last four decades, each representing a special policy measure implemented in each period. If the coefficients, the variances from the systematic and non-systematic risks, are the same the price volatility of each model can then be compared. In this case the price volatility in each period is mainly determined by the following coefficients:

$$\left(\frac{1}{a_1}\right)^2 \text{ from 1952 to 1972}$$

$$\left(\frac{1}{a_1 - b_1}\right)^2 \text{ for 1973}$$

$$\left(\frac{1}{a_1}\right)^2 \text{ for 1974 to 1976}$$

$$\left(\frac{1}{a_1 - b_1 + b_3}\right)^2 \text{ from 1977 to 1985}$$

As we can see the price volatility for the periods from 1952 to 1972 and from 1974 to 1976 are the same. The volatility for 1973 is not less than the above mentioned two periods if $b_1 \leq 2a_1$, and is less otherwise. The price volatility for the period from 1977 to 1985 is not larger than that of the period 1974 to 1976 if $2a_1 + b_3 \leq 2b_1$ and is larger otherwise. The price volatility of the period from 1977 to 1985 is not larger than that of the periods from 1952 to 1972 and from 1974 to 1976 if $b_1 - b_3 \geq 2a_1$. It will be the same if $b_1 - b_3 = 2a_1$.

7.4   EMPIRICAL EVIDENCE

The empirical evidence of the influence of policy measures on the price volatility of rice in Taiwan can be obtained in two ways:

1. First, the structural form of the models from 1952 to 1972 and from 1977 and 1985 can be estimated. The models for 1973 and from 1974 to 1976 cannot be estimated since there are only one and three observations respectively; and
2. Second, reduced equations for the price of rice can also be estimated for both models.

We are therefore going to estimate both the structural form of our models and the reduced equation for the price of rice.

We have two different sources of statistical data for estimating our econometric models, namely the data from the Food Bureau for the period from 1945 to 1985 and data provided by the National Chungching University in Taichung from 1966 to 1988. Though both data show similar developments there are small differences. We are therefore going to use these two sources of data separately. We have used the Data from the Food Bureau for the estimations calculated for the models 1952 to 1972 and 1977 to 1985 and with the data provided by the Chungching University for the model 1977 to 1988. A direct comparison of the estimated parameters with those derived with both the latter and the first data seems either meaningless or to be biased. Only the regression equations estimated with the Food Bureau data will be given in this section.

The Consumption of Rice and the Market Demand Function

Dependent Variable KOM – Estimation by Least Squares
Annual Data from 1952:01 to 1985:01

Usable Observations	34	Degrees of Freedom	30
Centred R**2	0.986361	R Bar **2	0.984997
Mean of Dependent Variable		1955.1815882	
Std Error of Dependent Variable		291.8110806	
Std Error of Estimate		35.7431900	
Durbin-Watson Statistic		1.418535	

	Variable	Coeff	Std Error	T-Stat	Signif
1.	Constant	−19.27415400	61.58677853	−0.312959	0.75647696
2.	HOPPP	6.60422178	2.76705195	2.386736	0.02350583
3.	PC 1981	−1.63096852	0.24690127	−6.605752	0.00000026
4.	KOM$_{t-1}$	1.00203175	0.02285635	43.840409	0.00000000

KOM . . . . .Total Consumption of Rice (m.t.)
HOPPP . . . .(Rice Price/Pork Price) 1,000
PC 1981 . . . .Per Capita Income At Constant Prices of 1981 (1.000 NT$)

All coefficients of both regression equations for the consumption of rice have the sign assumed in the derived microeconomic behavioural relationships. Because of the small size of the samples we do not consider all variables considered as influencing factors for the consumption of rice and market demand function as regressors in the above regression equations.

The regression equation estimated with data from the Chung-ching University shows the same results.

According to the regression equations estimated above we obtain the same 'surprising result' as we found in my last model (Chen, 1975), the Giffenian paradox of rice consumption in Taiwan.

Since in the above regression equation aggregate data are used the influence of the population (an exogenous variable) on rice consumption is not excluded. Another way to specify the consumption function is to estimate the per capita consumption function and then to define consumption by multiplying the per capita consumption by the population. The regression coefficients of the equation for the per capita consumption all have the theoretically expected sign.

Dependent Variable KOMP1 – Estimation by Least Squares
Annual Data from 1952:01 to 1985:01

Usable Observations	34	Degrees of Freedom	30
Centred R**2	0.992734	R Bar **2	0.992008
Mean of Dependent Variable		146.73703417	
Std Error of Dependent Variable		25.48258578	
Std Error of Estimate		2.27814812	
Durbin-Watson Statistic		1.456360	

	Variable	Coeff	Std Error	T-Stat	Signif
1.	Constant	9.33940030	11.17461196	0.835770	0.40989198
2.	HOPPP	0.50470557	0.17752345	2.843036	0.00796602
3.	PC 1981	–0.13918458	0.04490795	–3.099331	0.00419163
4.	KOMP1$_{t-1}$	0.91232674	0.05555029	16.423439	0.00000000

KOMP1 . . . .Per Capita Consumption of Rice (kgs)

The 'surprising results' of these regression equations might be due to the Giffenian character of rice consumption in Taiwan. According to the theoretical results derived in Appendix B, these results can be explained by the high average rice consumption in this period (about 163 kg per capita) and the ratio between the price of pork (representing the price of other foods) and of rice, which is about 7:1 on average in the period from 1952 to 1972 (the Food Bureau Data).

The average per capita consumption in the second sample (the Chungching University data) is about 120 kg while the price of pork and rice have a ratio similar to that used for the estimation in the first sample (the Food Bureau data).

According to the data provided by the Chungching University the per capita consumption has been reduced since the 1970s, but the ratio of the price of pork and rice has increased since the 1980s.

Thus the high share of rice consumption and the high ratio of the price of pork and rice may explain the Giffenian effect of the consumption of rice in Taiwan.

To test whether there was a structural change in the per capita consumption a Chow test was carried out. A significant structural change, however, could not be found.

Market demand is defined as the difference between total consumption and the consumption provided by the Food Bureau. $D_t = C_t - G_t$ and D_t: market demand, G_t: rice provided by the Food Bureau.

The Supply Function for the Model for 1952–72

Dependent Variable AN – Estimation by Least Squares
Annual Data from 1952:01 to 1972:01

Usable Observations	21	Degrees of Freedom	17
Centred R**2	0.968908	R Bar **2	0.963421
Mean of Dependent Variable	1502.4619048		
Std Error of Dependent Variable	312.9419059		
Std Error of Estimate	59.8523268		
Durbin-Watson Statistic	1.404919		

	Variable	Coeff	Std Error	T-Stat	Signif
1.	Constant	−765.4681380	731.7979598	−1.046010	0.31020213
2.	FEV1	−699.9498777	220.2752382	−3.177615	0.00550638
3.	ANBJ	2.8748812	1.0486710	2.741452	0.01391503
4.	TREND	36.8535141	4.5986160	8.014045	0.00000036

AN . . . . . . .Market Supply = Production minus amount collected by the Food Bureau
FEV1 . . . . . .Fertilizer Rice Exchange Rate
ANBJ . . . . .Planted Area for the Production of Rice

The market supply of rice is defined as the difference between the rice yield and the amount of rice collected by the Food Bureau. The regression equations estimated for market supply are different in the periods 1952 to 1972 and since 1977 because of the different policy measures in both periods. Both regression equations have the same sign as that derived in the microeconomic behavioural relationship given in Appendix A.

The Supply Function for the Model for 1977–85

Dependent Variable AN – Estimation by Least Squares
Annual Data from 1977:01 to 1985:01

Usable Observations	9	Degrees of Freedom	5	
Centred R**2	0.959584	R Bar **2	0.935334	
Mean of Dependent Variable		1684.0222222		
Std Error of Dependent Variable		158.9639564		
Std Error of Estimate		40.4236769		
Durbin-Watson Statistic		1.443090		

	Variable	Coeff	Std Error	T-Stat	Signif
1.	Constant	1798.215546	219.653251	8.186610	0.00044233
2.	PPA	1.241001	0.307461	4.036289	0.00995914
3.	PGAA	−107.713476	18.807337	−5.727205	0.00227120
4.	STEUER	1767.940779	688.561421	2.567586	0.05018213

PPA . . . . . .Price of Rice
PGAA . . . . .Support Price
STEUER . . .Landtax Rates given in Units of Rice

The supply of rice in the period from 1952 to 1972 does not depend on the price of rice in the way which was discussed above. The supply of rice in the period since 1977 cannot be estimated by using all variables specified by the theoretical consideration above because the samples from the Food Bureau and the Chungching University have only 9 and 12 observations respectively.

The supply on the market is negatively dependent on the support price because more rice will be sold to the Food Bureau if the support price is higher.

The Reduced Equations for the Price of Rice

Dependent Variable PPA – Estimation by Least Squares
Annual Data from 1952:01 to 1972:01

Usable Observations	21	Degrees of Freedom	17
Centred R**2	0.937649	R Bar **2	0.926645
Mean of Dependent Variable		278.36571429	
Std Error of Dependent Variable		91.83723191	
Std Error of Estimate		24.87325237	
Durbin-Watson Statistic		1.867582	

	Variable	Coeff	Std Error	T-Stat	Signif
1.	Constant	−72.1867348	105.8956621	−0.681678	0.50462437
2.	FEV1	81.3793361	83.8528709	0.970501	0.34540325
3.	TREND	9.3018991	3.9784534	2.338069	0.03186429
4.	PPA_{t-1}	0.4215900	0.2025452	2.081461	0.0528186

Dependent Variable PPA – Estimation by Least Squares
Annual Data from 1977:01 to 1985:01

Usable Observations	9	Degrees of Freedom	6
Centred R**2	0.967052	R Bar **2	0.956070
Mean of Dependent Variable		1021.5644444	
Std Error of Dependent Variable		203.1038950	
Std Error of Estimate		42.5697031	
Durbin-Watson Statistic		2.961236	

	Variable	Coeff	Std Error	T-Stat	Signif
1.	Constant	68.81471025	76.43676815	0.900283	0.40265627
2.	PGAA	78.66406876	10.71259314	7.343140	0.00032627
3.	PPA_{t-1}	−0.32871330	0.17032563	−1.929911	0.10185678

The regression equations for the reduced equation for the price of rice have the signs expected for their regressors.

For both of the reduced equations estimated with the samples from 1952 to 1972 and 1977 to 1985 (the Food Bureau Data) as well as 1977 to 1988 (the Chungching University Data) the OLS estimation of the non-systematical risks for the price of rice is used to estimate a sample variance of the random disturbances divided by the corresponding price in both equations.

The Price Volatility

The parameters which are relevant for the price volatility estimated in the above regression equation are as follows:

$$a_1 \approx 0.02$$
$$b_1 \approx 2.0 \text{ and}$$
$$b_3 \approx 0.5$$

According to the conditions studied above the price volatility in the period 1977 to 1985 must not be larger than that of the period 1952 to 1972.

An indicator for the price volatility can be found by estimating the standardized variance of the reduced equation for the price of rice in both periods. These are needed for comparison since the price of rice is not stationary.

The values of the standardized sample variances estimated for the periods 1952 to 1972 and 1977 to 1985 are 0.00913, 0.00110 respectively. Now an F-test for the calculation of the significance of the difference between the two estimated sample variances can be carried out. The F-value is equal to 8.3 Thus, this is an indicator for the influence of economic policy on price volatility with a significance level of 0.8 per cent.

In the case of the rice economy in Taiwan the estimated sample variance is higher in the period from 1952 to 1972 than in the last period. This may be due to the fertilizer–rice exchange programme implemented in the first period. In this case only the demand for rice is influenced by the market price whereas in the last period both the demand and supply of rice depend on the market price. Due to the reaction of both the supply and demand of rice the price volatility is smaller than that when the reaction solely occurs on the demand side.

We can summarize from the above theoretical and empirical investigations in this paper that the rice policy significantly influences the price volatility of rice in Taiwan.

7.5 SUMMARY

In this paper the influences of economic policy on the price volatility of rice in Taiwan have been studied. By deriving the microeconomic behavioural relationships for the supply and demand of rice the influences of policy measures since the 1950s in Taiwan have been studied and explicitly integrated into the theoretical consideration.

The fertilizer–rice exchange programme, the land tax payment in kind (rice), the sales of rice to the Food Bureau linked to the land tax and the support price programme are the most important policy measures to have been carried out since the 1950s.

According to the fertilizer–rice exchange programme the fertilizer – which is the most important input bought by the rice farmers in Taiwan – is supplied by the Food Bureau and must be paid for in rice. As a result of this policy the supply of rice does not depend on the market price of rice.

Since 1974 and the abolition of the fertilizer–rice exchange programme a support price programme for rice has been carried out. In the period from 1974 to 1976 there was no limit on the amount of rice that could be sold to the Food Bureau at the support price. Since 1977 the sale of rice to the Food Bureau at the support price has been limited to 970 kg per ha. Support prices for other crops have been implemented since the 1980s in order to reduce the production of rice. As a result of these measures the supply of rice depends among other things on the market price.

The consumption of rice displays a Giffenian character, i.e. it depends positively on its own price and negatively on income. A microeconomic theoretical explanation is given for this surprising empirical phenomenon.

Two models for the rice market have been estimated with statistical data from the years 1952–72 and 1977–85 by using the Food Bureau Data. The regression equations have the same sign as the coefficients expected on the basis of the theoretical considerations. For comparison data provided by the Chungching University from 1966 to 1988 are also used for estimating the model since 1977. There is no qualitative difference between the empirical results in using the Food Bureau data and the Chungching University data.

Our theoretical and empirical investigations propose a significant influence of economic policy on the price volatility of rice. The fertilizer–rice exchange programme seems to be mainly responsible for the higher price volatility of rice in Taiwan in the 1950s and 1960s.

APPENDIX A: DERIVATION OF UNDERLYING MICROECONOMIC BEHAVIOURAL RELATIONSHIPS FOR THE SUPPLY OF RICE

(The details of the following mathematical derivations are available on request.)

The goal of the rice farms can be regarded as the maximization of an income consisting of income from family labour forces, rents and rewards to capital subject to the constraints implied by the policy measures discussed in Section 7.2. In modelling the decision under uncertainty the utility is assumed to be a function of farm income.

As a result four underlying production models must be constructed, namely (1) a model for the 1950s and 1960s until 1972 when the fertilizer–rice exchange programme came to an end; (2) a model for 1973 after the termination of the fertilizer–rice exchange programme and before the introduction of the support price measure; (3) a model for the period 1974–76, a period in which the support price measure was carried out without a limit on the amount of rice which the farmers could sell to the Food Bureau at the support price; and (4) a model for the period since 1977 in which the support price is announced shortly before the planting season but the sale of rice from the farmers to the Food Bureau at the support price is limited to 970 kg per ha.

A7.1   The Production Model from the 1950s to 1972

The production model for rice in this period is characterized by the following points:

1. About 90 per cent of the farmers in Taiwan are land-owners. A farm is usually a family unit whose labour input consists of the labour forces of the family. In this period only a little capital was used in the agricultural sector. The only extraneous factor used by the farmer in Taiwan in this period was fertilizer. Therefore, the goal of the rice farmer in this period could be regarded as the maximization of farm income, which is the surplus of rice production after payment of fertilizer input.

2. The fertilizer for the rice production is solely supplied by the Food Bureau. The fertilizer price is given in units of rice and has to be paid in rice.

3. The land rent for tenants is limited to 37.5 per cent of the main crop per land yield. Therefore, it can be seen as the opportunity cost of land input. As a result of the regulations introduced by the land reform at the end of the 1940s the leasing of arable land can be neglected. Therefore, the land input for a farmer can be regarded as given. Due to the small average size of arable land used by the farms a farmer can only plant one crop. Therefore, the most profitable crop will be produced. This tends to be rice on the whole.

This gives an additional condition that must be fulfilled if rice is to be produced, namely

$$(4a) \quad EU\{(\overline{P}+v)[(\overline{Q}^*+u) - w_1 x_1^{*\prime}]\} \geq EU[(\overline{P}_i + v_i)(\overline{Q}_i + u_i) - w_{i1} x_1^*]$$

where $F_i = \dfrac{\delta F}{\delta x_i}$ derivative of F with respect to x_i

P_j : price of j-th crop with $\overline{P}_j$ as its expected price

$U(...)$: utility function

x_{ij} : i-th input for crop j

w_{i1} : fertilizer price for the i-th crop in currency unit

$\overline{Q}$: planned (expected) output

In the formal model for derivation of the rice farmers' behaviour we assume:

1. The farmers maximize expected utility, which is a function of income.

2. The utility function is characterized by constant absolute risk aversion, with *r* being the coefficient of absolute risk aversion.

3. The random fluctuations in the production function and price are assumed to be additive, and the random variables are assumed to be independently normally distributed.

4. The production function, i.e. the function relating the planned output and input, is assumed to be twice differentiable with decreasing marginal returns for a single factor. Three factors, fertilizer, labour and land, are considered explicitly. The input of insecticide will not be considered because its use depends on

the weather conditions and reduces the yield fluctuation due to the different climate in each period.,

The rice production model for the land-owner

The land owning farmers' income is defined as:

$$(\overline{P} + v)[F(x_1, x_2, x_3) + u - w_1' x_1]$$

where $P = \overline{P} + v$: the price of rice; $\overline{P}$ = expected price of rice. Since there is no risk of ambiguity the subscripts representing a farmer are dropped in the interests of simplicity.

$\overline{Q} = F(x_1, x_2, x_3)$ production function; $\overline{Q}$ = planned output

x_1 : input of fertilizer

w_1' : fertilizer rice exchange rate

x_2 : labour input

x_3 : land input

v, u : additive random variable $E(u) = E(v) = 1$ and Var(u) and Var(v) are given, u and v are assumed to be stochastically independent.

The expected utility can be specified as follows:

$$\overline{P}\,\overline{Q} - \overline{P} w_1' x_1 - \tfrac{1}{2} r[\overline{P}^2 \, \mathrm{Var}(u) + \overline{Q} - w_1' x_1)^2 \, \mathrm{Var}(v)]$$

where Var(...) denotes the variance of the random variable in bracket;

r : the coefficient of absolute risk aversion.

The first order conditions are:

(1a) $(F_1 - w_1') [\overline{P} - R_1] = 0$ where $R_1 = r(\overline{Q} - w_1' x_1^*) \mathrm{Var}(v)$, i.e.

$\quad\;\; F_1 = w_1'$ or $\overline{P} = R_1$

(2a) $F_2(x_1^*, \overline{x}_2, \overline{x}_3) \geq w_2 / (\overline{P} - R_1)$

(3a) $\overline{P} \geq R_1$

$\quad\;\; 2r(Q - F_1 x_1^*) > 0$ risk premium

w_2 : wage rate in the individual sector in currency unit

x_i : available amount of i-th input for the farmer.

The second order conditions for maximization are assumed to be fulfilled.

The first order condition (1) is similar to the usual condition of decisions under certainty because the fertilizer price is set at the fertilizer–rice exchange rate in units of rice.

An important consequence of the above theoretical foundation is that the price of rice is not included in the supply function of rice and demand function for fertilizer.

The rice production model for the tenants

Although most farmers in Taiwan are land-owners there are still some tenants. Therefore, we also have to derive their behaviour:

The tenant's income is defined as:

$$(\overline{P} + v)[0.625(\overline{Q} + u) - w_1' x_1]$$

because the tenant has had to pay a share 37.5 per cent of the crop yield as rent since the land reform in Taiwan.

The first order conditions corresponding to the land owner case are:

(1b) $F_1(x_1^*, \overline{x}_2, \overline{x}_3) = w_1' / 0.625$

(2b) $F_2(x_1^*, \overline{x}_2, \overline{x}_3) \geq w_2 / (0.625\overline{P} - R_2)$

where $R_2 = 0.625r(F - w_1' x_1)V$

(3b) $\overline{P} \geq R_2$

The second order conditions are assumed to be fulfilled. In comparison to the land-owner model three first order conditions for the maximization of the tenants income are multiplied by 0.625, which is the share of the crop yields after deduction of the rent which has been set at 37.5 per cent of the main crop yield since the land reform.

Therefore, the tenant's supply function for rice and his demand function for fertilizer conform to those of the land-owner with the exception that the constant term has to be corrected by 0.625 and $R_1 > R_2$. As we don't have any statistical data for the rice production of the land-owners and the tenants we will use aggregated production data. From the above microeconomic behaviour we believe that the aggregation error should not be considerable since the fertilizer demand function is similar in both cases and the other first order conditions seem to be fulfilled in the form of inequality constraints.

Remark: Production models for tenants were also constructed for the other relevant policy regimes. They are left unregarded in this appendix for the sake of brevity but are available on request.

A7.2   The Production Model for 1973

The year 1973 was characterized by the deregulation of the fertilizer and rice markets in Taiwan. Although the Food Bureau still supplied fertilizer in this year other private suppliers were also allowed to sell fertilizer to the farms. Additionally, the farmers did not pay for fertilizer in rice. The Food Bureau lost an important source for obtaining rice from the farmers and subsequently the farmers had to pay a land tax in rice. This and rice purchased on the market represent the two ways used by the Food Bureau to collect rice in 1973. As a result the share of the rice holding of the Food Bureau fell from a third of the rice production in the 1950s and 1960s to 9 per cent in 1973.

During the economic development in the last two decades the share of agricultural labour and of the tenants have fallen but the main features of the agricultural sector have nevertheless remained largely unchanged. We can now construct the following formal production model for rice in 1973:

The rice production model for the land-owner farmers
The land-owning farmers' income from the rice production given in currency units is:

$$(\overline{P} + v)[F(x_1, x_2, x_3) + u] - w_1 x_1$$

where w_1 is the fertilizer price in currency units and the other symbols have the same meaning as in Section A7.1.

The first order conditions for maximization are:

(5a) $F_1(x_1^*, \overline{x}_2, \overline{x}_3) = w_1/(\overline{P} - R_3)$ where $R_3 = r\overline{Q} \ \mathrm{Var}(v) > 0$
(6a) $F_2(x_1^*, \overline{x}_2, \overline{x}_3) = w_2/(\overline{P} - R_3)$
(7a) $\overline{P} \geq R_3$

Compared to the corresponding first order conditions in Section A7.1 the fertilizer input will be lower in the model for 1973 and, therefore, the expected rice yield must also be lower for 1973 if the same expected price for rice and the same fertilizer price are given in both cases.

The most important result from the comparison of both models in Sections A7.1 and A7.2, and in this section is that the supply of rice in the latter model positively depends on the expected price of rice while it is independent of the price in the first model.

A7.3 The Production Model for the Period 1974–76

The most important feature for the production model in this period is the support price measure for rice. The support price is announced before the planting season. There is no limit on the sale of rice from the farmers to the Food Bureau at the support price. The fertilizer is sold by the Food Bureau and the price is given in units of the New Taiwan Dollar. The farmers can pay for the fertilizer in either rice or currency.

The land-owner model

The land-owner's income from the production of rice is defined as:

$$g(\overline{Q} + u) - w_1 x_1$$
where g: the support price

In this case there is no price risk.

The first order conditions are:

$$(9a) \quad F_1(x_1^*, \overline{x}_2, \overline{x}_3) = \frac{w_1}{g}$$

$$(10a) \quad F_2(x_1^*, \overline{x}_2, \overline{x}_3) \geq \frac{w_2}{g}$$

$$(11a) \quad F_3(x_1^*, \overline{x}_2, \overline{x}_3) \geq 0.375\overline{Q}$$

These results are similar to those of the production model under certainty.

A7.4 The Production Model Since 1977

A special feature characterizes the main difference between the models from 1974 to 1976 and since 1977. While there is no limit on the amount of rice which can be sold to the Food Bureau at the support price in the model from 1974 to 1976 the Food Bureau limited this amount to 970 kg per ha in 1977.

The land-owner model

The land-owning farmers' income from the production of rice is defined as:

$(\bar{P} + v)(\bar{Q} - \pi x_3 + u) - w_1 x_1 + g\pi x_3$　or

$(\bar{P} + v)(\bar{Q} + u) + \pi(g - \bar{P} - v)x_3 - w_1 x_1$

where π : farmers' sales limit per acre to the Food Bureau
　　　　　at the support price

　　　g : support price

We assume : $g \geq \bar{P}$, i.e. the support price should not be lower than the expected market price.

The first order conditions are:

(13a)　$F_1(x_1^*, \bar{x}_2, \bar{x}_3) = w_1 / (\bar{P} - R_5)$, where $R_5 = r(\bar{Q}^* - \pi x_3^*) \, \mathrm{Var}(v)$

(14a)　$F_2(x_1^*, \bar{x}_2, \bar{x}_3) \geq w_2 / (\bar{P} - R_5)$

(15a)　$(\bar{P} - R_5)F_3(x_1^*, \bar{x}_2, \bar{x}_3) \geq 0.375\bar{Q}^* + \pi(\bar{P} - g - R_5)$

　　　　$x_3 > 0$

The above first order conditions (13a) and (14a) gives the surprising result that only the expected market price of rice is relevant for the farmers' decision.

The first order condition (15a) is for the acreage input in the production of rice with the result that the support price for rice is relevant for the decision on land input when producing rice. Since acreage is indispensable in the production of rice the supply of rice and the fertilizer input are also functions of the support price.

Amount of rice obtained by the Food Bureau

The amount of rice obtained by the Food Bureau (T_t) is equal to the rice sold under the support price measure and the land tax paid in rice, i.e.

$T_t = \pi^* x_{3t} + \beta_t x_{3t}$

where π^* : share of rice sold under the support price measure

　　　$\bar{\pi} \geq \pi^* = 0$

　　　$\bar{\pi}$: sale quota per planted acreage under the support price measure

　　　β_t : land tax rate (in unit of rice)

Since the farmers can choose between selling rice of up to sale quota per acreage to the Food Bureau according to the support price measure or on the market, they may decide to sell an optimal amount of rice to maximize their net revenues. The farmers have to carry rice to the so-called total representatives of the Food Bureau if they sell it under the support price measure. If they choose to sell rice on the market the transport is taken over by the trader. Therefore, only in the first case do the farmers have to bear the transport cost and the net revenue of an industrial farmer can be defined as:

$$P_t(Q_t^* - \pi x_{3t}^*) + \pi g_t x_{3t}^* - \frac{1}{2} s(\pi)^2 x_{3t}^*$$

where $s(\pi)^2 x_{3t}^* / 2$ is the transport cost for delivering rice to the Food Bureau.

The decision of the farmer on the amount of rice to be sold to the Food Bureau under the support price measure is the maximization:

$$\text{Max } [P_t(Q_t^* - \pi x_{3t}^*) + \pi_t g_t x_{3t}^* - \frac{1}{2} s(\pi)^2 x_{3t}^*$$

$$\text{subject to } \overline{\pi} \geq \pi^* \geq 0 \quad Q^* \geq \pi_t x_{3t}^*$$

The solution of the above maximization problem is equal to:

$$\pi^* = \left(\frac{g_t - P_t}{s} \right)$$

Thus

$$\pi^* = 0, \quad \text{if } P_t \geq g_t \quad \text{or}$$

$$\pi^* = \frac{g_t - P_t}{s}, \quad \text{if } g_t > P_t \text{ and } \overline{\pi} \geq \pi^*$$

The amount of rice obtained by the Food Bureau is equal to:

$$T_t^* = \left(\frac{g_t - P_t}{s} + \beta_t \right) x_{3t}^*$$

where $(\pi + \beta_t) x_{3t}^* \geq T_t^* \geq \beta_t x_{3t}^*$

Assuming that rent is equal to:

$x_{3t}^* = \alpha_3 \overline{Q}_t^*$ where $\overline{Q}_t^*$ is the planned yield and $1 > \alpha_3 > 0$. Now the amount of rice obtained by the Food Bureau can be specified as:

$$T_t^* = \alpha_3 \left(\frac{g_t - P_t}{s} + \beta_t \right) \overline{Q}_t^*$$

APPENDIX B: THE FUNCTION OF PER CAPITA RICE CONSUMPTION

We assume for simplicity two food varieties, say rice and pork, which are needed in a functional relationship given as:

$$F = F(C_1, C_2)$$

to satisfy the food demand of a person, where F is assumed to be given, F is 'food consumption' and C_i is one of the two food varieties. Taking over the work from Spence (1976), Dixit and Stiglitz (1977) and Helpman and Krugman (1985) F can be compared to the subutility function. In the short-run F is assumed to follow the habit of food consumption, i.e. $F(C_{1t}, C_{2t}) = m\ F(C_{1t-1}, C_{2t-1})$ where m is a parameter for adjusting food consumption habits. For simplicity m is assumed to be equal to 1. The budget equation for the consumption of food is:

$$P_1 C_1 + P_2 C_2 = Y$$
where P_i : consumer price of the food variety i
Y : food budget

The combination of both food varieties to satisfy both the food subutility and the budget equation under consideration of the habits of food consumption is:

$$dC_{1t} = \Gamma[(dY_t - C_{1t}dP_{1t} - P_{2t}\frac{F_1}{F_2}dC_{1t-1}) - (C_{2t}dP_{2t} + P_{2t}dC_{2t-1})]$$

where $\Gamma = P_1 - \frac{F_1}{F_2}P_2$ and $F_i = \frac{\delta F}{\delta C_i}$ for $i = 1, 2$

$$C_{2t}dP_{2t} + P_{2t}dC_{2t-1} = (1+n)C_{2t}dP_{2t}$$

with $n = \dfrac{P_{2t}}{C_{2t}}\dfrac{dC_{2t-1}}{dP_{2t}}$ which can be interpreted as the 'demand elasticity of pork'. We assume $n < -1$.

From the above equation the demand for the first food variety, say rice, is negatively dependent on income (food budget) as well as on the second food variety (say pork) and positively on the price of rice if:

$$\Gamma < 0, \text{ or } P_1 < \frac{F_1}{F_2}P_2$$

REFERENCES

Chen, John-ren (1971): 'An investigation and prediction of the production, consumption and market of rice in Taiwan', Taipei (in Chinese), National Chengchi University.

—— (1975): 'Produktion, Konsum und Markt des Nahrungsmittels Reis in Taiwan – ökonometrische Untersuchung und Prognose' in *Zeitschrift für die gesamte Staatswissenschaft*, 439–87.

—— (1993a): 'A generalization of modelling for markets of substitutive raw materials – effects of introducing new good in the volatility of price and trade volume of the gross substitutes', *Seoul Journal of Economics*, **7** (3), 267–81.

—— (1993b): 'Economic policy and producer's behavior: a study of the behavior of the rice farmer in Taiwan', Working Paper Internationale Ökonomik, University of Innsbruck.

—— (1993c): 'The demand of rice in Taiwan: a Giffen paradox?', Working Paper Internationale Ökonomik, University of Innsbruck.

Dixit, A. and J.E. Stiglitz (1977): 'Monopolistic competition and optimum product diversity', *American Economic Review*, **67**, 297–308.

Grossmann, G.M. and E. Helpman (1991): *Innovation and Growth in the Global Economy* (The MIT Press).

Helpman, E. and P.R. Krugman (1985): *Market Structure and Foreign Trade* (Harvester Press).

Huang, T.-C. (1987): 'The Four Decades Food Policy' in Taiwan, Taipei, (in Chinese), mimeo.

Newbery, D.M.G. and J.E. Stiglitz (1981): *The Theory of Commodity Price Stabilization: A Study in the Economics of Risk* (Oxford).

Spence, M.E. (1976): 'Product selection, fixed costs and monopolistic competition', *Review of Economic Studies*, **43**, 217–36.

Turnovsky, S.J. (1983): 'The Determination of Spot and Futures Prices with Storable Commodities', *Econometrica*, **51**, 1363–87.

8. Trade Liberalization, Domestic Price Instability and Commodity Futures Markets: The Case of Potatoes

Wyn Morgan, A.J. Rayner and C.T. Ennew

8.1 INTRODUCTION

Output and price variability are inherent features of temperate and tropical soft commodities. The problems created by output and price variability are exacerbated for perishable crops; the inability to store the crop across seasons and the potential deterioration within seasons precludes the reduction of inter-seasonal price and income instability by stockholding. In the developed world, the presence of output and price variability in agricultural commodity markets has typically attracted some form of government intervention that has had stabilization as either a direct or indirect objective. However, as many developed country governments begin to question the wisdom of large expenditures on the agricultural sector and the extent of intervention is reduced, the industry may have to look for alternative mechanisms to deal with the problem of instability. Forward contracts have a long history within the agricultural sector as a means of guaranteeing a certain price for a certain quantity of output and thus reducing the instability experienced by the individual trader. However, in the context of reducing instability such contracts do have disadvantages, most noticeably that they lack flexibility. The alternative is futures trading that provides a more flexible and liquid means of managing the problems of instability within an agricultural commodity market.

This paper examines the role of futures markets in providing a means of reducing the instability associated with a perishable soft commodity, namely potatoes. The context for this analysis is the gradual reduction in the extent of market intervention and in particular, the lifting of import restrictions. Section 8.2 provides a general overview of the potato market in Great Britain while Section 8.3 examines the relationship between trade liberalization, instability and futures trading. In Sections 8.4 and 8.5 we examine the role of the futures market in providing a reduction in price instability by focusing specific attention on both the price discovery and risk management functions of the market.

8.2   MARKET BACKGROUND

Maincrop potatoes represent one of the less stable of the range of temperate agricultural products. A high degree of variability in yields (relative to competing crops) is translated to a high degree of variability in prices, and despite common perceptions, the limited support buying programmes, which operate in the domestic market, provide little reduction in intrinsic price variability (Ennew *et al.,* 1985). Maincrop potatoes are produced seasonally but have discontinuous inventories, which can compound the problem of yield variability. Production decisions are made in the spring and the harvest occurs in the late summer/autumn. Inventories are seasonally large just after the harvest but most of the stock is sold by the beginning of June. Movements in the spot price reflect the pattern of seasonality in a predictable manner: prices rise from the autumn through to June in order that costs of storage are covered (both direct costs and deterioration in store). Moreover, the average price in the marketing season is largely determined by the size of the harvest in relation to stable demand.

Potato policy in Great Britain is implemented by the Potato Marketing Board (PMB) in consultation with the government, and seeks to reduce intrinsic market instability.[1] Since 1955, the main instruments employed have been area quotas to control planned production, support buying to provide a price floor to the market and, until 1979, import controls to protect domestic producers against foreign competition.

Before 1979, self-sufficiency formed the crux of intervention arrangements: the government operated a price guarantee system combined with the power to impose import controls in years when domestic harvests were adequate to meet domestic requirements at 'reasonable prices'[2]. However, the latter policy contravened EC trade regulations, and import controls were removed at the end of the transition period for the accession of the UK to the EC. This resulted in a major disturbance to the status quo in the British market. Existing market support arrangements could no longer be continued since there was now the possibility that the PMB, through its intervention purchases, would act as 'buyer of last resort' for the EC potato crop (Marsh, 1985). British policy could be undermined via import penetration despite the substantial natural protection afforded by the costs of transporting potatoes from the continent to Southern England. Support policy was subsequently modified: area quota policy has been implemented more rigorously,[3] support buying has been limited in volume and the price floor used as a safety net rather than to underpin the market and the government has disengaged itself from the stabilization scheme.

8.3   LIBERALIZATION, INSTABILITY AND FUTURES TRADING

Most agricultural commodity markets are characterized by intrinsic price instability. Interventionist agricultural policy in the industrialized countries usually has domestic price stabilization as a major objective (Winters, 1989). The prevalence of the stabilization objective can be explained by reference to the gains to farmers, the group in the domestic economy with the dominant interest in stable prices (Tyers, 1990). The reduction in domestic price variance is frequently obtained by the use of trade instruments, such as variable levies, which sever the link between domestic and border (trade) prices. The domestic market is thereby insulated or shielded from world market conditions and fluctuations in international prices. In some instances, the domestic market is isolated totally from international market volatility via the employment of binding import quotas or through the pursuit of domestic self-sufficiency. Underlying the actions of policy-makers in such cases may be the (hidden) belief that trade gives rise to greater domestic price variability than isolation of the domestic market.

Using a simple 2-country partial equilibrium model, Greenaway *et al.,* (1993) suggest that the variability of agricultural commodity prices under free trade and autarchy depends on the relative size of supply variances for the trading partners and the degree of correlation between supply disturbances. Since, by assumption, yield variance is identical in both countries, the relative size of the supply variances depends upon the area planted in each country. This model allows price variability under various policy scenarios to be compared with price variability under free trade for an importer (country 1) and an exporter (country 2). Thus, for example, it can be shown that a policy of complete price stabilization in country 1 will reduce domestic price variability to zero at the cost of increased price variability in country 2; price insulation through variable trade taxes has similar results, reducing variability in country 1 and increasing it in country 2. The case of free trade relative to autarchy is more complex. The greater the correlation between the supply disturbances, *ceteris paribus*, then the greater the variability of price in both countries under free trade. However, as the area planted in country 2 increases relative to country 1, free trade increases price variability in country 1 but decreases variability in country 2. Finally, as the price response coefficient in country 2 increases relative to country 1, free trade will reduce variability in country 1 and increase variability in country 2 (Greenaway *et al.,* 1993).

Although it is difficult to identify empirically which of the above situations applies in the case of the British potato market, the relatively high correlation in yield disturbances (Morgan, 1991) and the relative size of the British market relative to the EC as a whole (around 14 per cent of EC production) suggests that the British market may provide an example of a situation in which free trade might be expected to increase price variability. That is to say, from a theoretical perspective, the removal of the import ban on potatoes in 1979 will have increased price variability in the British market and reduced price variability in European markets.

Such an outcome was widely anticipated at the time this change was implemented (Young, 1978). The domestic potato market was expected to display a greater price variability consequent upon free trade and the correspondingly reduced role that could be played by the PMB in stabilizing the market.[4] In the absence of stabilization provided by government intervention, two obvious alternatives presented themselves for agents wishing to reduce the risk associated with producing and trading in potatoes, namely forward contracts and futures trading.

Forward trading provides a mechanism for reducing price variability in that both parties can agree a price in advance and guarantee that price for a set quantity of the commodity. However, such contracts also have a number of limitations. Forward markets are not organized in any way and trading can take place at any time and any place, thus both parties will incur costs associated with searching for a suitable trading partner and forming an agreement on price. As a direct result of the lack of organization, quality levels will vary across contracts. Also, as the trade is in the physical commodity, direct inspection of the commodity is necessary if trade is to take place, which is time consuming and costly. Price levels will be uncertain as there is no uniformity in the way individuals bargain, which means that the market is limited in its ability to disseminate information to traders. As there is no centralized market or exchange where the contracts are drawn up, there is no mechanism to ensure that the contract is delivered at the time specified, resulting in possible litigation and lack of trust. There may be an imbalance in the number of buyers and sellers, representing the possible frustration of aspirations and a waste of resources in the fruitless search for contracts. Finally, the lack of price discovery that is always a feature of forward markets, means that speculators are effectively excluded from the market, thus causing problems of liquidity.

Futures trading provides an alternative mechanism for managing the variability and risk associated with producing and trading commodities. In very simple terms, futures trading is an organized and highly liquid form of trading in forward contracts. As such, it offers users the benefits associated with forward pricing without the constraints implied by the need to make a physical transfer of the commodity. The need for futures markets can be questioned when forward contracts can play a similar role. Telser (1981) suggests that although the reduction of risk can be achieved by the use of forward contracts, these are less flexible and fungible than futures contracts, which may make them less attractive to non-commodity traders (i.e. insurers). The liquidity of the futures market and its standardized contract make it a highly fungible market. As a result of its liquidity, it can be suggested that the ability of futures trading to offer a convenience yield is as important if not more so than its risk management features.

Nevertheless, the risk reducing opportunities provided through futures trading mean that such mechanisms are increasingly being seen as a means of providing the individual grower or trader with a means of reducing the price variability they face in the absence of more formalized systems of market intervention. Concern over price variability provided an impetus for the establishment of the London Potato Futures market in 1980: futures trading was envisaged as a means of providing price stability for agents through the opportunity for hedging.[5] The market was introduced on the understanding that price variability would increase and that futures trading could counteract the effects of this variability.

The ability of futures markets to reduce the risks associated with price variability and stock holding through hedging is probably their most widely recognized role. The apparent ability to reduce the risk of stock holding through hedging arises because spot and futures prices move together, so losses in one market can be offset by gains in the other. However, as Gray and Rutledge (1971) realized, any attempt to eliminate risk altogether by hedging is virtually impossible as that would require the spot and futures markets to move perfectly in parallel. This tends not to be the case, even in markets that are functioning effectively and thus the producer or merchant can only hope to reduce risk; the closer the relationship between spot and futures prices, the greater the risk reduction (Paul *et al.*, 1981). In fact, Kamara (1982) suggests that pure risk avoidance hedging is not a goal of trading on modern futures markets as hedging is motivated by a desire to stabilize income and partially to increase profit, thus introducing an element of speculation into any trading strategy. Further, he argues that in a non-storable commodity, there is no functional relationship between spot and futures price although there is some degree of positive correlation.

A precondition for effective risk reduction is the ability of the futures market to act as a predictor of future spot prices ensuring that the basis narrows as contracts reach maturity. This is described as the price discovery function of futures trading (Edwards, 1981). Futures markets are able to perform a price discovery function for two reasons. First, trading on such markets and the resultant prices are seen as a clear indication of the collective expectations of market traders regarding future supply and demand conditions at contract maturity. Second, because the markets are essentially paper markets, prices can react quickly and relatively costlessly to changes in information. If the resultant price changes are an accurate reflection of the information reaching the market, then the market is an efficient processor of information.

Furthermore, if the resultant price changes are considered to be an accurate reflection of future supply and demand conditions then they will exert an influence on inventory decisions; falling futures prices would indicate that future demand is expected to be lower and/or future supply is expected to be higher. This would in turn induce inventory holders to reduce stock leading to lower current spot prices. If this is the case, then the futures market is an efficient disseminator of information. This information flow is not simply one way; to the extent that current spot prices are in some way an indicator of inventory decisions, they will provide futures traders with a source of information regarding future supply and demand conditions. We should also note that, as Gray and Rutledge (1971) point out, for a perishable commodity such as potatoes, price discovery will really only be effective in the post harvest season (although we can, in principle, extend this to consider periods when the size of crop is likely to be known). This point is reiterated by Kofi (1973) in his comparative study of wheat and potato futures markets in the US. The results of this analysis suggested that market efficiency is far weaker in non-storable commodity markets: *'all things being equal, the allocative and forward pricing function of futures markets will be more reliable for continuous than for discontinuous inventory markets'* (p. 585).

Although the forward pricing and risk management properties of futures markets are thought to be weaker for perishable commodities than for non-perishable commodities, there remains the potential for futures trading to provide some reduction in instability, at least within a season, if there exists a close relationship between spot and futures prices for the relevant commodity. The following section examines these aspects of the futures market for potatoes in Great Britain.

8.4 ANALYSING THE EFFECTIVENESS OF FUTURES TRADING IN POTATOES

For a futures market to be an effective mechanism for risk reduction, it must perform the price discovery function. The ability of the futures market to act as a predictor of future spot prices depends upon the quality of information flows between the two markets. This in turn will be influenced by both the volume of trade and by the nature of the futures commodity relative to the spot commodity. Adequate trading volumes are necessary to eliminate the wild price fluctuations that may exist in thin markets and a close relationship between the futures commodity and the spot commodity is required if agents in the market are to view the futures price as representative of the spot price.[6]

Given the importance of price discovery the first stage in any analysis of the effectiveness of the LPFM requires an investigation into its ability to perform the price discovery function. If a futures market is performing its price discovery role efficiently, then any fluctuations in spot and futures prices should be positively correlated to reflect this flow of information. In the case of the LPFM, empirical work to date has tested the efficient markets hypothesis (Sheldon, 1987) and the effectiveness of hedging strategies (Entwhistle, 1987). To date, the ability of the market to perform its price discovery role has not been evaluated in any detail.

The concept of price discovery implies that the futures price embodies all available information and thus is the best predictor of the future spot price. Evidence on the extent to which future prices respond to market information is provided by Ennew *et al.,* (1993) who show that market prices are responsive to relevant information such as quota decisions and yields. This analysis can be extended to examine more explicitly the ability of the futures market price to predict future spot price. This analysis is conducted over the period of the markets operation, using 35 data points (9 years by 4 delivery dates except May 1981 where no trading was operative). The specific objective is to examine the ability of the futures price 4 months prior to delivery ($F_{T-4,t}$) in month T in the marketing year t to predict the spot price at contract maturity ($S_{T,t}$).

Univariate analyses of the time series shows that they had comparable time series properties. Specifically, they both contained *deterministic* 'seasonal' components (relating to delivery) and neither contained either a non-seasonal unit root or a unit root at a seasonal lag.[7] In other words, both series could be represented as comprising seasonal means plus stochastic components that were stationary in levels and across delivery dates. Thus, a necessary condition for market efficiency, that of comparable time series properties, is met by the futures and spot price series.

The deterministic component was removed from both series and the stochastic component of $S_{T,t}$, ($ES_{T,t}$) was regressed on the stochastic component of $F_{T-4,t}$, ($EF_{T-4,t}$).[8] The predicted values from the regression were added to the relevant deterministic components to give the predicted spot price values $SH_{T,t}$. Figure 8.1 shows these predicted values against the actual spot prices $S_{T,t}$. It is clear that there are two aberrant periods – April and May of 1983/84 and of 1987/88 – but that otherwise the predictive ability of the information contained in the futures price is quite reasonable.[9] In 1983/84 spot prices in April–May were substantially above levels that could be predicted from futures contracts struck earlier in the season but this might have arisen from an abnormally low yield giving rise to high prices in that season. For 1987/88, spot prices in April and May were substantially below levels that could be predicted from prior futures contracts. This divergence was sufficiently large as to

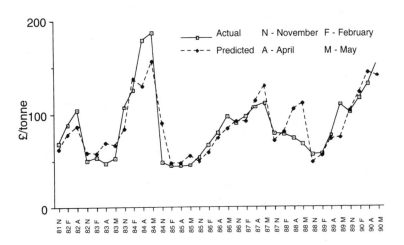

Figure 8.1   Actual and predicted spot prices

provoke an investigation into trading behaviour and calls for the suspension of trading due to fears that the market had been cornered. Subsequent investigation revealed no irregularities. A possible explanation for the occurrence of this situation lies with the reduced volume of trade in that season, in combination with imports which were higher than normal for this stage of the season. If this was the case, then it is interesting to note that the higher level of imports was not reflected in lower futures prices and this may suggest some problems in relation to information flows onto the futures market.

While the analysis above suggests that futures prices on the LPFM have generally acted as reasonable predictors of future spot prices, further analysis of the risk management role of the market is required. In particular, there is a need to consider the overall impact of the LPFM on price variability as well as a more specific evaluation of the hedging performance of the market.

As argued in Section 8.2, there is a strong theoretical case to suggest that inter-seasonal price instability would increase in the British market as a consequence of liberalizing trade in potatoes. At the same time, it can be argued that the introduction of futures trading might be expected to reduce inter-seasonal price instability. Since both of the events occurred virtually simultaneously, it is difficult to disentangle the relative effects of futures trading and free trade. Nevertheless, a comparison of inter-seasonal price instability pre- and post-1980 is instructive. Furthermore, supporting evidence may be gleaned from an examination of price variability in Europe, given that theoretical arguments suggest that an increase in price variability in Britain as a consequence of liberalizing trade would be accompanied by a reduction in price variability in Europe. Table 8.1 reports a simple coefficient of variation for prices for five countries for the periods before and after trade liberalization. The table also reports the ratio of the coefficient of variation in price to the coefficient of variation in yield. The latter measure may be more reliable since it controls for the effects of yield variability[10] in a systematic fashion, whereas the simple coefficient of variation only controls for yield variability by the exclusion of outlying observations. Hypothesising that liberalizing trade would increase variability in Britain and reduce variability in Europe, but that the introduction of futures trading in Britain may offset the trade induced increase in variability then we would

Table 8.1   Means and coefficient of variation (CV) of domestic prices[a]

Period	Britain	Belgium	France	Germany	Holland
Raw CV[b]					
1969–79	0.32	0.35	0.27	0.18	0.35
1980–90	0.23	0.44	0.35	0.25	0.35
Yield adjusted					
1969–79	5.07	4.17	4.29	4.28	6.80
1980–90	3.12	4.71	4.29	1.88	3.56

Notes:
(a)   The deflator used is the GDP deflator (1985 = 100) and all prices are annual averages as supplied by Eurostat.
(b)   Excluding 1976 as an outlier.[11]

expect to find evidence of a reduction in price variability in Europe and also in Britain. The results from an examination of the simple coefficient of variation on real price are counter to what might have been expected. The figures indicate a reduction in variability in Britain in the period following the removal of the import ban and the introduction of futures trading, and an increase in variability elsewhere in Europe. However, when the ratio of price variability to yield variability is considered, there is some support for the basic hypothesis in that there is evidence of a reduction in price variability in Britain, Germany and Holland, with only Belgium showing signs of increased price variability.

It may be worth noting that given the existence of area control in the British market, inter-seasonal pricing will be underpinned by the knowledge that there are unlikely to be substantial variations in plantings and thus the role of the futures market in guiding price formation across seasons may be somewhat limited. Accordingly, it might be expected that the impact of futures trading on inter-seasonal price variability will be relatively small.

However, the futures market may play a more significant role in relation to intra-seasonal price variability. Price instability within seasons arises partly as a consequence of variable demand patterns, but primarily as a consequence of variations in quantities available to the market at any one point. The impact of trade liberalization on intra-seasonal price variability is unclear. However, given that free trade removes any certainty about the total supply to be moved in any given season, there is an intuitive case for arguing that liberalizing trade may increase price variability. Furthermore, given that the production cycle is basically the same for all northern European producers, the opportunities for imports to reduce price variability by smoothing out supply changes across season is limited. By the same token, it is arguably in relation to intra-seasonal pricing that the futures market for a perishable commodity will display its most significant risk reducing properties. However, this outcome is by no means certain.

Through the process of arbitrage, a futures market will be linked to the cash market for a commodity. However, the introduction of futures trading will not necessarily decrease price volatility in the spot market. Conceptually, speculators add liquidity to the market so allowing spot traders to hedge and price variability to be smoothed. Speculation itself can stabilize prices if speculators buy when prices are low and sell when prices are high (Friedman, 1953). However, if speculators respond to price movements, buying/selling only after prices have changed then volatility may be increased (Baumol, 1957). The introduction of a futures market might be expected to improve the price discovery mechanism – the processing of information with regard to price determination. Consequently, the price efficiency of the spot market might be expected to increase. However, spot market volatility might increase if futures markets are distorted by technical factors or manipulation, or suffer from a lack of liquidity or agents investing in futures are not well-informed (Figlewski, 1983).

Provided we are prepared to assume that liberalizing trade does not reduce intra-seasonal price variability, the risk reducing properties of the LPFM can be examined through an analysis of the behaviour of spot market prices pre- and post-1980. The data set consisted of weekly cash prices from September to May for each of the production years 1969–91. The null hypothesis of a unit root for the spot price within the marketing season was not rejected for practically all years.[12]

A monthly volatility series was constructed based on the Figlewski (1983) measure:[13]

$$s_{it} = \left(\sum_{j=1}^{n_{it}} \left(p_{itj} - p_{itj-1} \right)^2 / n_{it} \right)^{\frac{1}{2}} \tag{1}$$

where s_{it} is the (Figlewski measure of) volatility in month i in (production) year t

p_{itj} is the price in week j in month i in (production) year t

n_{it} is the number of weeks in month i in (production) year t

Given substantial inter-seasonal price variability, this series was divided by average monthly price to give a 'normalized' price volatility measure akin to a coefficient of variation, v_{it}.

$$v_{it} = s_{it}/p_{it}$$

where p_{it} is average price in month i in (production) year t.

Table 8.2 lists mean values for v_{it} by month for the period 1969–79 prior to the futures trading and the period 1980–91 after the introduction of futures trading. It is apparent from these figures that volatility varies across the different months of the marketing season, being higher at the beginning when information concerning the size of the crop is under evaluation and at the end when imports of 'new' potatoes affect the market. However, the aggregate picture indicates that normalized spot price volatility is lower in the latter period.

The simple analysis of average levels of volatility may only give a partial insight into the degree of price variability pre- and post-1980 and this again is due to the need to incorporate the effects of yield variability in a systematic fashion. There tends to be an association between yield and the quality/storability of the crop. Years

Table 8.2 Mean and standard deviation of v_{it}

| | 1969–79 | | 1980–91 | |
	Mean	St. Dev.	Mean	St. Dev.
Sept.	0.072	0.028	0.043	0.026
Oct.	0.059	0.033	0.043	0.038
Nov.	0.027	0.016	0.020	0.001
Dec.	0.024	0.021	0.027	0.032
Jan.	0.047	0.032	0.022	0.020
Feb.	0.035	0.026	0.017	0.013
Mar.	0.050	0.043	0.019	0.015
Apr.	0.060	0.040	0.045	0.039
May	0.106	0.079	0.042	0.022
Average	0.053	0.035	0.031	0.023

in which yields are low (and prices high) may be characterized by a higher degree of price volatility than years in which yields are high, simply because of the poor quality of the crop and the greater potential for deterioration in store. Thus to accommodate such effects it may be appropriate to examine the relationship between volatility and the price level and the *a priori* expectation would be that a positive relationship would exist between the two. In order to investigate this possible link, the logarithm of volatility was regressed on the logarithm of price and monthly dummy variables;

$$\ln v_{it} = \beta \log p_{it} + \sum_{i=1}^{9} \theta_i D_i$$

where $i = 1 \ldots 9$ denotes each month in the marketing season from September to May.

Table 8.3 presents estimates of this equation for the full sample period 1969–91 while Tables 8.4 and 8.5 present estimates for the two sub-samples 1969–79 and 1980–91. The F statistic is 3.9 for the Chow test of the null hypothesis that the coefficients are identical

Table 8.3   OLS estimates 1, 1969–1991

Dependent variable = $\ln v_{it}$ Regressor variable	Coefficient	t-ratio
$\ln p_{it}$	−0.04	−0.54
D_1 (Sept.)	−2.86	−8.34
D_2 (Oct.)	−3.02	−8.75
D_3 (Nov.)	−3.77	−10.81
D_4 (Dec.)	−3.91	−11.10
D_5 (Jan.)	−3.53	−9.90
D_6 (Feb.)	−3.81	−10.71
D_7 (Mar.)	−3.60	−10.01
D_8 (Apr.)	−3.12	−8.52
D_9 (May)	−2.76	−7.49

$\bar{R}^2 = 0.18$	$DW = 1.68$
$\hat{\sigma}^2 = 0.81$	$SSE = 129.0$

Heteroscedasticity tests	Test statistic	DF	Critical value 5%
B-P-G	11.6	9	16.9
ARCH	0.05	1	3.8

Table 8.4   OLS estimates, 1969–1979

Dependent variable = $1nv_{it}$		
Regressor variable	Coefficient	t-ratio
$1np_{it}$	0.24	−2.53
D_1 (Sept.)	−3.53	−9.07
D_2 (Oct.)	−3.83	−9.79
D_3 (Nov.)	−4.64	−11.70
D_4 (Dec.)	−4.83	−12.03
D_5 (Jan.)	−4.16	−10.22
D_6 (Feb.)	−4.49	−11.06
D_7 (Mar.)	−4.17	−10.12
D_8 (Apr.)	−3.99	−9.47
D_9 (May)	−3.43	−8.17

$\bar{R}^2 = 0.27$ $DW = 2.18$
$\hat{\sigma}^2 = 0.54$ $SSE = 47.97$

Heteroscedasticity tests	Test statistic	DF	Critical value 5%
B-P-G	3.9	9	16.9
ARCH	1.5	1	3.8

in the two sub-samples. The 5 per cent (1 per cent) critical value from the F-distribution with (10,187) degrees of freedom is 1.83 (2.32) so that the null is rejected and the models for the two sample periods are considered to be superior to a single model for the whole period.

The sub-sample regressions are acceptable in that the relevant diagnostics do not reject the null hypotheses of no autocorrelation and homoscedasticity.[14] Both suggest that there is a significant and positive relationship between the level of price volatility and the level of price. A comparison of the regression parameters across the sub-samples indicates that price volatility is lower in the period 1980–81 than in the period 1969–79. The response of volatility to price is also diminished in the second sub-period compared to the first sub-period.

8.5   CONCLUSIONS

Futures trading provides an alternative to forward contracting or

Table 8.5   OLS estimates 1, 1980–1991

Dependent variable = $\ln v_{it}$ Regressor variable	Coefficient	t-ratio
$\ln p_{it}$	0.19	0.96
D_1 (Sept.)	−4.12	−4.72
D_2 (Oct.)	−4.16	−4.74
D_3 (Nov.)	−4.87	−5.51
D_4 (Dec.)	−4.99	−5.56
D_5 (Jan.)	−4.90	−5.44
D_6 (Feb.)	−5.13	−5.71
D_7 (Mar.)	−5.06	−5.57
D_8 (Apr.)	−4.36	−4.72
D_9 (May)	−4.20	−4.46

$\bar{R}^2 = 0.16$	$DW = 1.93$
$\hat{\sigma}^2 = 0.77$	$SSE = 58.75$

Heteroscedasticity tests	Test statistic	DF	Critical value 5%
B-P-G	12.9	9	16.9
ARCH	0.95	1	3.8

government intervention as a means of managing the risk associated with producing and trading in soft commodities. The risk management and risk reduction functions of a futures market are, however, dependent on the ability of that market to provide a forum for price discovery. The price discovery features of a futures market are generally considered to be greater for storable than for non-storable commodities, although this does not mean that futures markets for non-storable commodities cannot perform forward pricing and resource allocation functions. An analysis of the forward pricing and risk reducing properties of the London Potato Futures Market provides evidence of some success in forward pricing and risk reduction, although in the latter case, the effect is most noticeable within rather than between seasons.

However, the LPFM is by no means an ideal market. Some of the more obvious market distortions have been discovered in this paper and there is a body of evidence that highlights problems in the market relating to quality specifications (Anderson, 1989), production and storage hedging (Ennew *et al.*, 1992) and institutional mystique/lack of awareness (Ennew and Morgan, 1991). Despite these problems, the evidence presented in this paper suggests that in aggregate terms, futures trading has had some success in risk reduction. In that context, there may be a role for futures trading as a mechanism for stabilization in relation to a variety of other soft commodities. However, if such a system is being considered as an alternative to intervention or forward contracting then it is clearly important to ensure an institutional framework that encourages clear links between spot and futures prices. Furthermore, given the mystique surrounding futures trading (Paul *et al.*, 1981), there is a clear need to provide active encouragement to growers and merchants to use futures markets in order to ensure the necessary volume of trade to allow the market to function effectively.

NOTES

1. Note that the potato crop, unlike other major agricultural commodities is not covered by a Common Agricultural Policy regime so that intervention is left in the hands of the governments of member states.
2. In practice, an import ban was imposed in the majority of years prior to 1979. In addition, imports were small in years of low domestic harvests.
3. Essentially, area quota is adjusted downwards to offset an upward trend in yields and producers are dissuaded from planting in excess of their quota via the threat of excess area levy payments.
4. Subsequent analysis of policy intervention (Ennew *et al.*, 1985) has shown that the modified support buying arrangements provided little reduction in intrinsic price variability.
5. For an analysis of the LPFM see Ennew *et al.*, (1992).
6. Differences in quality between spot and futures markets are a cause of concern in relation to the LPFM. The more stringent quality specification employed by the futures market will inevitably drive a wedge between futures and spot price. However, if the quality premium is constant, this wedge need not detract from the price discovery and risk management functions of the market.
7. A variable X_t is said to be integrated of order (d, D) denoted by $X_t \sim \mathrm{I}(d, D)$ if the series requires differencing d times and seasonally differencing D times to make it stationary. The Augmented Dickey–Fuller (ADF) unit root test and the Dickey–Hasza–Fuller (DHF) seasonal unit root test were employed to test for stationarity. The test statistics are available from the authors.
8. The prior removal of seasonal means enforces a zero constant on the regression. The regression corrected for first order serial correlation (rho = 0.3) was:

$$ES_{T,t} \quad = \quad 0.63 EF_{T-4,t} \qquad R^2 = 0.70$$
$$(6.5)$$

9. This presupposes that traders would be informed as to the deterministic components (delivery date means).

10. Since a policy of area control operates in the GB market, the main source of price variability is the variability in yield.
11. Both 1975 and 1976 were characterized by severe drought in Europe, with the result that potato yields were unusually high. However, given that Eurostat data is provided only on an annual rather than a crop year basis, only 1976 was identified as an outlier.
12. The hypothesis that the weekly price series within the marketing season had a unit root was rejected at the 10 per cent level for only the 1973, 1975 and 1986 production years.
13. If the price series is a random walk, $p_{itj} = p_{itj-1} + u_{itj}$, then the measure of volatility is simply the standard deviation of the residuals.
14. The series $\ln v_{it}$ and $\ln p_{it}$ were also examined for non-stationarity for each sub-sample. Residual series $\ln \tilde{v}_{it}$ and $\ln \tilde{p}_{it}$ were constructed from regressions of $\ln v_{it}$ and $\ln p_{it}$ on the nine monthly dummy variables. The relevant Dickey-Fuller statistics for the residual series were ;

D-F STATISTICS

Variable	Period	D-F Statistic
$\ln \tilde{v}_{it}$	1, 1969–1979	–8.25
$\ln \tilde{p}_{it}$	1, 1969–1979	–4.84
$\ln \tilde{v}_{it}$	1, 1980–1991	–10.08
$\ln \tilde{p}_{it}$	1, 1980–1991	–16.12

The residual series are stationarity and relevant regressions are

$$\ln \tilde{v}_{it} = 0.24 \ln \tilde{p}_{it} \quad i,t = 1,\ 1969\text{–}1979 \quad \bar{R}^2 = 0.07 \quad DW = 2.18$$
$$(2.66)$$

$$\ln \tilde{v}_{it} = 0.19 \ln \tilde{p}_{it} \quad i,t = 1,\ 1980\text{–}89,\ 1991 \quad \bar{R}^2 = 0.01 \quad DW = 1.93$$
$$(1.01)$$

REFERENCES

Anderson, J. (1989): 'Letter to the editor', *Agra Europe Potato Markets Supplement*, 1 September.

Baumol, W.J. (1957); 'Speculation, profitability and stability', *Review of Economics and Statistics*, 263–71.

Edwards, F.R. (1981): 'The regulation of futures markets: a conceptual framework', *Journal of Futures Market*, 1 (suppl.), 417–39.

Ennew, C.T. and C.W. Morgan (1991): 'A survey of attitudes to and patterns of use on the London potato futures market', Report for the London Potato Futures Association, London.

Ennew, C.T., C.W. Morgan and A.J. Rayner (1992): 'Objective and subjective influences on the decision to trade on the London potato futures market', *Journal of Agricultural Economics*, **43**, 160–74.

Ennew, C.T., A.N. Jennings, A.J. Rayner and G.V. Reed (1985): 'British stabilisation policy in a European context', *Journal of Agricultural Economics*, **29**, 43–60.

Entwhistle, G. (1987): 'Evaluating hedging strategies on the London potato futures market', paper presented to the Agricultural Economics Society Annual Conference, University of Reading.

Figlewski, S. (1984): 'Futures trading and volatility in the GNMA'. *Journal of Finance,* **36**, 445–6.

Friedman, M. (1953): 'The case for flexible exchange rates', in *Essays in Positive Economics,* Chicago (UCP).

Gray, R.W. and D.J.S. Rutledge (1971): 'The economics of commodity futures markets – a survey', *Review of Marketing and Agricultural Economics,* **39** (4), 57–108.

Greenaway D., C.W. Morgan, A.J. Rayner and G.V. Reed (1993): 'Trade liberalisation and domestic price instability in an agricultural commodity market', *Applied Economics,* **25**, 199–205.

Kamara, A. (1982): 'Issues in futures markets', *Journal of Futures Markets,* **2**, 261–94.

Kofi, T.A. (1973): 'A framework for comparing the efficiency of futures markets', *American Journal of Agricultural Economics,* **55**, 584–94.

Marsh, J. (1985): 'Economics, politics and potatoes: the changing role of the potato marketing board in Great Britain', *Journal of Agricultural Economics,* **36**, 325–43.

Morgan, C.W. (1991): 'Great Britain's potato stabilisation policies and the European market', unpublished PhD thesis, University of Nottingham.

Paul, A.B., K.H. Kahl and W.G. Tomek (1981), 'Performance of Futures Markets: The Case of Potatoes', USDA, Economics and Statistics Service, Technical Bulletin no.1636.

Sheldon, I.M. (1987): 'Testing for weak form efficiency in new agricultural futures markets', *Journal of Agricultural Economics,* **38** (1), 51–64.

Telser, L.G. (1981): 'Why there are organised futures markets', *Journal of Law and Economics,* **24** (1), 1–22.

Tyers, R. (1990): 'Trade reform and price risk in domestic and international food markets', *World Economy,* **13**, 212–29.

Winters, L.A. (1989): 'The so-called non-economic objectives of agricultural policy', *OECD Economic Papers,* **13**, 237–66.

Young, N. (1978): *A British Potato Futures Market: A Preliminary Appraisal* (University of London, Wye: Centre for European Studies).

Index